# FOLLO

# Jesus

# INTO JAIL

BY

## Shannon Teichmann

*Following Jesus into Jail*

Trilogy Christian Publishers
A Wholly Owned Subsidiary of Trinity Broadcasting Network
2442 Michelle Drive, Tustin, CA 92780

Trilogy Christian Publishing/TBN and colophon are trademarks of Trinity Broadcasting Network.

For information about special discounts for bulk purchases, please contact Trilogy Christian Publishing.

*Trilogy Disclaimer: The views and content expressed in this book are those of the author and may not necessarily reflect the views and doctrine of Trilogy Christian Publishing or the Trinity Broadcasting Network.*

Manufactured in the United States of America

10 9 8 7 6 5 4 3 2 1
Library of Congress Cataloging-in-Publication Data is available.

ISBN: 978-1-63769-846-4
E-ISBN: 978-1-63769-847-1

# TABLE OF CONTENTS

# INTRODUCTION

In the wee hours of the morning of June 28th, 1969, a tumultuous storm rumbled off the Gulf of Mexico and traveled over Houston, Texas, causing power outages. The backup generators at St. Joseph's Hospital ran as I came crying into this world at 2:53 a.m., according to my mother. I often wondered if this was portentous of my life, full of storms, seeming failures, depression, anxiety, fear, and great shyness. Coming to know God through His son, Jesus Christ, who has become my Lord and Savior, changed that a few short years ago, making me wish that happened much sooner in life. Perhaps substantial heartache could have been avoided, or maybe suffering led to being saved and fully committed to following Christ.

Yet sometimes, I worry I even failed at being a "true follower" of Christ. The first year of new birth was wonderful but was followed by what seemingly were the worst of mistakes of my life. Conceivably, Satan may have attacked me viciously to derail me from my newfound salvation and commitment to Christ. Maybe I let him and fell too easily. Before I get to that, I will begin with my childhood and younger years, fraught with fear.

My first memory is from the crib, the first formative one I can recall, which I describe in words now, although this is difficult since I lacked language then. The best I can do is translate from feelings and wonderment. I was crying in a dimly lit room, bathed in soft, golden light. I was upset without knowing why. A woman's face appeared over the crib rail. I looked up in wonder as a man joined her, handing me a bottle, putting its nipple in my mouth. Everything was mystifying: *What was this place? Who were these people? How did they know what I needed? How did I know to suck on the nipple, to drink, to be satisfied?*

My next memory finds me standing up in my crib pushed against the wall, the room's light switch accessible, which I am flipping up and down. Miraculously, the room's light is turning off and on, delighting me. Someone near me barks, "Shannon, quit that!" I look over, and the order comes from a girl who is standing next to a boy. They are rolling paint onto the walls. The boy laughs at the situation. He has written something on the wall, much to the girl's consternation. She yells at him to stop writing profanity on the wall. I did not understand who they were, but soon would as the next earliest memory finds the family sitting around the dinner table. My father addresses them by name, Lisa and Chris, and the concept of "family" dawns on me. We are a "family": this is my sister Lisa, brother Chris, completed by mother and father. This epiphany makes this memory stand out, as in one moment of time it all comes together, who these people are: I am their child, a part of their family.

In my next memory, the theme of fear emerges. I'm a toddler standing at the wall, using it as my canvas as I color with my crayons. Someone sees what I am doing, probably one of my well-meaning siblings, perhaps my brother, who I later realize seems to enjoy getting me into trouble. I am in my element, loving the colors and lines I create, not knowing that what I am doing is "wrong," but my father quickly responds, yelling at me to "quit that!" He spanks my rear end hard enough to hurt. I burst into tears. This moment teaches me to fear wrongdoing. *What happens when I fail to realize what I am doing is wrong? How will*

*I know ahead of time?* From this, I learn to be very cautious, and in turn, my journey into crippling shyness begins.

Next, I remember drawing on paper, having learned my lesson, apparently. I am at the kitchen table. My mother asks me what I am drawing. I do not look up at her or meet her in the eye out of fear that I am drawing something "wrong" and I may be punished. When she insists that I explain, I do so almost inaudibly: "There are two planets, this one is earth, and the other one is Uncle Bill's planet, and he is walking across the bridge joining the two to visit us." Mom's youngest brother, Bill, was visiting us at the time. I remember her saying to Uncle Bill something along the lines that I was an imaginative child.

I began drawing as soon as I could hold a pencil. My artistic creations became my escape into another world, my therapy. Drawing eased my anxiety throughout childhood and teenage years. Artistic creation became one of two passions from a young age that I hoped to pursue as an occupation. The other is writing. If I was not drawing, I was keeping diaries and attempting stories or plays. I never actually finished a story or a play save for one of each as favors to friends, one at age twelve, the other at sixteen. Art and writing were sources of joy and comfort.

---

I grew up in a household fraught with tension. I sensed everyone's unhappiness. My parents fought daily. My father yelled, and my mother pacified, doing what she could to keep the peace. I perceived that she loved him very much and feared losing him. I sensed that she placated him out of desperation to prevent losing him. The situation kept her nervous and irritable. She worked at respectable positions with great responsibility. She was a creative, skilled writer. During my childhood, she wrote a work of fiction, never published, and it kept her "high strung." She disliked being disturbed when typing or deep in thought. I remember approaching her at her typewriter, trying to get her attention. I cannot recall what was so urgent, but as shy and fearful of punishment as I was, it must have been important enough for me to dare to interrupt her, but I sure regretted it, after uttering, "Mom, Mom, Mom… Mom, Mom…" until she suddenly sprang out of her chair, screaming at me, "What? I'm working! Can't you see that?" and charging at me. I turned around and ran fast away, bawling, hoping to avoid a spanking. When Mom spanked me, it was not hard, it did not hurt physically as Dad's belt spankings did, but the emotional hurt was worse. I learned the hard way to never disturb her at the typewriter after that, no matter the circumstances.

My shyness worsened, but my parents did not see how much until they put me in public school. Prior to the first grade, I did well enough in kindergarten. No unpleasant memories of it stand out to me, just arts, crafts, and gentle caregivers. Only nap time emerges from my memories as unpleasant. I never could sleep and sometimes was gently chastised if I whispered to a child nearby. First grade was another matter. I was terrified. Mrs. Sarapak was my first first-grade teacher, and she was fearfully stern, easily irritated, and a commanding presence. Daily, I sat at my desk praying to avoid her notice, but one fateful day she called on me, and I was so panicked that I stood up when I was supposed to simply answer a question while remaining seated. She was upset that I was standing. She told me to sit back down. However, paralyzed by fear, I mutely stood there.

Soon after, something unusual occurred. She called me out of the room, and I obediently followed her and another woman to a very small room. Mrs. Sarapak left me alone with this stranger, dressed in a white lab coat like a doctor would wear. The woman held up a picture of a fireman and asked me, "What is this?" I was so confused. The answer was obvious. *Why was she asking me this? Did she truly not know? If I told her what that was, would I be showing her up? Did the poor woman truly not know?* The situation frightened me. I just looked at my feet, refusing to meet her eye. She proceeded through several more pictures that I thought if a person could not identify them, they were probably dumb.

Soon after that, Mrs. Sarapak pinned a note to my dress and told me to make sure that my parents received it, emphasizing how important it was for me to not lose it. Obediently, I took the task seriously, walked directly home, just as instructed, and delivered the note to my parents as soon as they arrived home from work. I do not remember their reaction as they read the note. I probably did not stick around to see but retreated to the haven of my bedroom. The next day at school, Dad came to my classroom and called me out and took me home early. Mom was waiting at home, and they sat me down in the living room and explained that I would not be going back to school. I was aghast. I remember protesting, saying that I wanted to go to school. As scared as I was, I still wanted to be there. I implored them to change their minds, but they simply said, "You are not ready. You will go back to kindergarten and start first grade next year." I later learned that the note explained to my parents that I was "retarded" and needed special education. Such was the misdiagnosis of my severe shyness. My dad remembers this incident very well; it made him so mad. He knew there was nothing wrong with my intellectual capability. I am amused contemplating this now as someone who eventually earned a bachelor's degree magna cum laude and a master of library science summa cum laude. After my parents withdrew me from the first grade and returned me to kindergarten, I adjusted to the wait, and when I started first grade again the following year, I had a different teacher, Mrs. Griego, who was kind, gentle, and always smiled. I did not fear her.

These early events set the tone for my upbringing. I performed poorly academically in elementary school because of my severe shyness, but I got through it, although there was little social interaction. My shyness continued in my teen years. In fact, it was pervasive to age forty, although it lessened over time. I was unpopular during my primary education. Eventually, I communicated better with teachers, learning to trust them, and my grades improved. As a teenager with few friends and no social life, I threw myself into my studies. While I did not excel on a regular basis, I did well overall.

---

I experienced traumas as a teenager that I never fully dealt with therapeutically. I did not disclose them to anyone for many years. I buried them and moved on. My physique prompted them. My chest size quickly grew enormous, beginning to show in elementary school. By the time I was twelve, I was in a full C cup. A year later, I wore D cups, attracting unwanted attention from boys. Harassment began in middle school after my parents divorced and my mother remarried, moving with my stepfather from Albuquerque, New Mexico, to Olathe, Kansas. My parents' friends lived on a lake in Gardner, Kansas, and often visited them on weekends. When they headed home Friday evening, they left me for the weekend, returning to pick me up on Sunday.

The family's daughter was two years younger than me. I spent time with her the most. They had several sons, the youngest two years older than me at fourteen. None of their sons gave me problems, but one time the youngest son's friends cornered me, proposing I go with them as a group onto the adjacent golf course to make out with each of them. Their proposal dismayed me. *How could they think I would agree to do that?* I refused, and they made a move toward me, but I got away from them even though they cornered me. They must not have been serious; they easily could have stopped my flight. The daughter was away spending the night with a friend; otherwise, I thought she surely would have prevented this encounter.

Another time I was unlucky the summer I turned fourteen. The girl was home on this occasion. Rather than intervening on my behalf, she instigated the situation. The family had neighbors so close they shared a driveway. The neighbors' sixteen-year-old nephew was visiting from Colorado. Immediately, he was attracted to me and bothered me throughout the day. He would not leave me alone no matter how rude I was to him; I was so annoyed. Late in the night, the girl had the brilliant idea to sleep in the back of her dad's pickup truck. The boy from next door, of course, continued to pester me. I was miserable. I failed to realize she wanted something to happen. To this day, I have no idea what motivated her. I was weak and naive. Looking back, I can easily say I should have just refused to sleep outside, but I did not know what the night had in store.

We were both trying to sleep while the sixteen-year-old nagged me, "Just take a short walk with me to talk, that is all, then I'll leave you alone, I promise!"

I kept saying, "No," "Get lost," "Forget it," "Leave me alone," etc.

Finally, the girl said, "Oh for God's sake, Shannon, just take the walk, get it over with, and he will leave you alone! I want to sleep!" (expletives included).

I sighed in resignation and agreed, walking with him up the driveway. He led me across the road onto the golf course, out quite a ways. Funny thing, he didn't speak at all. We stopped, and I looked up into the clear night, breathed in fresh summer air, took in the stars, and began to think, *This isn't so bad*, when suddenly I found myself ground pinned under him. He tried to force me to french kiss and put his hands under my clothes. In sheer panic, I struggled, kicked, tried shoving him, to no avail. Finally, I startled him enough to back off, and I screamed, "Help! Rape!" repeatedly, which stunned him, so he let me go.

I jumped up and ran for my life, faster than I ever had before, all the way off the golf course, across the road, down the driveway, straight into my friend's house as he tailed me the entire way, hollering, "Wait! Stop!" I slammed the door, locked it, and in continued fear, ran into my friend's room, locked her door, and fell onto her bed, sobbing. The entire episode horrified me. Soon there was knocking on the door, a voice calling,

"Shannon! Are you all right?" I realized it was the youngest son. He added, "I heard your cry, call for help, went to investigate, and saw you running from the golf course. What happened? Are you okay?" I answered that I was and said no more. I didn't want to talk about it. I think he guessed. At least, I hoped he knew. I remember thinking, *I hope he kicks his butt!*

I never shared this experience with anyone. I remember early the next morning, at 6 a.m., calling my stepdad, pleading with him to come pick me up immediately. Ralph knew I was desperate to return home, so he drove over directly to get me. He did not question me, which I respected because I felt too ashamed to talk about it, as though I were the one to blame for the incident. I never trusted the girl again. I was cautious on subsequent visits. I never saw the sixteen-year-old from Colorado again, thankfully.

A similar incident occurred with a boy from my Alateen group, which I attended after my mother decided that Ralph was an alcoholic. She announced it to me out of the blue one night and informed me that henceforth, she would be attending Al-Anon meetings, and I, Alateen. We went to these meetings for two years, from 1982 to 1984. During this time, I befriended a few of the group's teens. One boy was a year younger than me. Given his age, youthful face, and overall sweet demeanor, plus his similar situation at home with one of his parents being alcoholic, I liked him as a friend. I trusted him; unfortunately, I should not have, as he tricked me one time on a bike outing. He convinced me to meet him at an arcade, to which I biked from my house and he his, meeting in the middle, as we lived on opposite sides of the town. He was with one of his friends. After playing games at the arcade for a while, he convinced me to bike over to his house under the pretense of meeting his mother. On the way, his friend left us and biked away to his own home. I remember thinking, *That is odd.* More odd was arriving at his house to find no one home. He insisted that I come in; his mother would arrive home any time. I wish I had not fallen for his ruse. This was still my fourteenth summer, after the lake episode. If only I could have known better. I should have known better. Victims often blame themselves, though. He was unsuccessful with his attempts with me, thankfully. I got away from him as I had before but still felt assaulted. I was devastated because I thought he was a sincere friend; he was a year younger than I! When I arrived home, I was in trouble as I had ridden too far and was gone too long. My parents grounded me for two weeks after severely lecturing me. I took my punishment silently. I never spoke of this incident, either, to anyone for many years.

Other episodes occurred at school. One boy pursued me quite a bit, but his intentions were obviously lascivious, and I avoided him as much as I could. He harassed me in art class unbeknownst of the teacher. I felt ashamed of the mistreatment, blamed myself, and stayed silent about it. Another event occurred with a girl, incredibly. She really scared me. I invited her over one time. We were alone in the den, my mother shut away in her "office" upstairs, writing out of earshot. The girl pinned me down and accused me of being a lesbian. I didn't understand what that meant. I had no clue such a thing existed, so naive and sheltered. Thereafter, I felt terrified of her and avoided her completely. She became angry with me, feeling rejected, so she threatened to beat me up after school. I believed her, so I went to the principal's office to report her threats. I did not tell them about her unwanted advances in my home. They called her into the office with me and questioned her. She admitted she wanted to beat me up because I had cut off our friendship. At that point, they excused me. I am unsure what they said to her, but we never spoke again, and she left me alone thereafter. Many close calls, but I survived them without too much damage and felt lucky and blessed that I was not hurt worse.

Other tumultuous related events happened later in my teens through my nineteenth year of life. I never dealt with any of these events therapeutically in an official capacity, either through counseling or, at least, confession, until I was well into my twenties and only then by discussing them in a limited manner with very few people. Being overdeveloped physically was unfortunate. Social interaction with boys proved impossible because they focused on my physique. They were uninterested in me as a person, friend, human being. I was only an object, until I met the man who became my first husband. I did not win women over easily, either because they were jealous or envious of my shape if they were small chested, or they simply distrusted me because of it. The few female friends I made saw past it and my shyness and truly cared about me. Fortunately, by the age of twenty-two, I took the opportunity to resolve the issue physically and never have once regretted the surgery that normalized my size, freeing me from chronic shoulder and back pain as well as social ostracism.

---

Despite my teenage troubles, I achieved academic honors through rigorous study easily by lacking a social life. I attended college, perhaps not the best decision, but an endeavor I undertook at my mother's behest, who long dreamed of a college education for herself. Since that never materialized, she insisted that I fulfill her dream by proxy. I desired to attend art school. I reasoned that I could make money through commercial art, even possibly clothing design, since I was always designing clothing for women, sketching out unique concepts. My parent's perspective was that anyone in the arts could not actually make a living unless phenomenally talented and/or well-connected, neither of which I was. Art and writing would have to wait half a century. I dutifully attended college, not majoring in fine art, for which my heart longed.

My mother wanted me to major in business. She was a brilliant woman with a savvy head for business, but me—not so much. I had neither the mind for economics nor the interest. I found mathematics and sciences inherently boring, and I was not smart enough to grasp much of it. I excelled at algebra and statistics, but that is about it in the "harder sciences." I discovered I loved history and languages, doing very well in them. With foreign languages, when written, I learned to read and write quite well and earned high marks, but I could not understand them aurally or pronounce them in the foreign accent convincingly enough for teachers and professors I studied under to encourage me to major in them. I am a visually-oriented person. I felt lost as to what to study and what to do with my life. I knew growing up from childhood through high school and into college that my true dream and calling was to be a wife, mother, artist, and writer. I even wrote as much under my high school yearbook senior biography, and those passions never changed. My parent's hopes and dreams superseded mine because my individual personality was weak, lacking willpower. I was obedient, dutiful, desiring my parents' love and approval. I lived to obey and to please, not just them, but others I really cared about in my life. My parent's wishes even superseded my first husband's.

When I married, my first husband's wishes should have been more important to me, but I was not raised as a traditional Christian, wherein traditional gender roles as described in God's Word were unsupported in our household. My mother was a feminist. Women should work, be independent, and do what they want to do, regardless of what the husband thinks or says. If a husband cannot support what a wife wants, the wife should leave him and either stay single or find another, more compatible man. When I told Mom I was getting married, she supported it and loved my first husband, but she told me under no circumstances was I to quit college, regardless of his wishes. I had to build a career and stand on my own two feet. I know she had my best interest at heart. She said that I should be able to leave him and live independently at any given time should he cheat on me, fail to support me, or, heaven forbid, die. I had to be a career woman. She was sorely disappointed that I chose not to major in business, but at least I stayed the course and attended college until I earned a bachelor's degree. What I chose to major in, however, was a big mistake.

I was raised in a household with parents who believed in New Age philosophies and were fairly anti-traditional Christians, believing Jesus to be a good man born to "show humanity how to become one with God," but otherwise "survived the cross, got married to Mary Magdalene, had children, and that the crucifixion was the greatest ruse ever perpetrated on earth." Ironically, my mother prayed the Lord's Prayer daily, and any time she meditated or gave psychic readings, and truly loved Jesus for His teachings, but she did not believe that He was God incarnate... Yet, she also believed in His healing power and ability to protect, teaching me to "surround myself with the white light of Jesus Christ" at all times. *Seems a bit contradictory.* In college, I figured out that we were "eclectic." We took what we thought was the best from every religion, philosophy, or spirituality and rejected the rest. I fully adhered to what my parents taught me. I was proud of it as well, to reject the traditional patriarchy, suppression of women, and I condemned Christian "religious fanatical, fundamentalist, judgmental Bible-thumpers." My birth father taught me this as well as my mother before 1984, the year he became a born-again Christian. Thereafter, my mother and Ralph had greater influence on me, as my father lived in another state. Sadly, he and I were estranged for decades, mostly my fault, being so obstinate as to avoid hearing him talk about Jesus in an effort to help save me. Thank God we reconciled over ten years ago and have since enjoyed a loving, close father/daughter relationship.

---

When I met sociology in college, it was a natural fit. This discipline greatly reminded me of Ralph, so smart, politically astute; he would have excelled in it, as I did since I parroted my parents. Since I could not make a living as an artist and author, I became a sociologist (which did not happen after college), the "next best thing." Once I realized there was not much of a market for sociologists in the workplace, aside from the lucky few who become statisticians for the federal government, I could teach it. I set my heart on that in my junior year. I took the academic theoretical track as opposed to the practicum; instead of signing up for internships, I signed up for a senior thesis. This helped me develop research and writing skills and, eventually, publication and public speaking via conference presentations. This was the proper path to graduate school to earn a master's and a doctorate.

The more immersed I became in social studies, naturally leading to women's studies and feminism, the more incompatible my husband and I grew. He was unhappy. We loved each other greatly. More than likely, I loved him more. I was madly, desperately in love with him. At the same time, I was deeply insecure as I had been from life's beginning. I never developed a healthy self-esteem. I battled weight problems from the age of thirteen, in addition to gigantomastia. I became needy and clingy. These traits led me to become a smothering presence. When my husband told me to quit college and work full time, I refused. He never said that immersing myself in social issues including environmentalism, feminism, social stratification, racism, vegetarianism, and animal rights bothered him, but I believe it must have.

While he was politically moderate, he was in the Navy. I realize how embarrassed he must have felt while he was away at sea, and I sent him care packages slapped with Greenpeace stickers all over the box. What can I say? I attended a public college, and for the past forty or fifty years, they have become well-known liberal indoctrination centers.

Sadly, our differences grew, and I did not compromise. I valued my parent's wishes more than my husband's. Our marriage lasted four years, ending when he met someone else with whom he was more compatible. I was heartbroken, devastated; it took me years to recuperate, many more to understand all that went wrong and what I could have done differently if I knew then what I eventually learned. However, regret over the situation is useless and unneeded. I moved on, especially after I became pregnant with someone else. Today I cannot imagine a world without my son, who I love to impossible depths. I would die for him. Such is a mother's love. He is my greatest joy. I am so proud of him and blessed that God let me be his mother, a role I most likely did not deserve. When I was younger, I thought I would be the best mother because I would love and cherish him and make him the center of my world. I would do whatever it took to raise him to be confident and have good opportunities in life to pursue his dreams. I could have been a better mother. My love for him is endless, but I made many bad decisions out of a selfish need to be "happy." If I was not "happy," things had to change because I had to be happy. My happiness mattered more to me, at times, than others'. I say this now from the Christian viewpoint, being saved, desiring only to please God. I should give myself a break, but that is difficult. As I look back on the years, my heart breaks over and over again for the purely selfish things I did, and I think, *If only...* Mostly, my heart breaks for the ones I broke. I know God forgives me and wiped the slate clean when I asked Him to come into my heart as my Lord and Savior. If only I could be as forgiving and gentle with myself as He is me.

---

As a teenager, I felt a close connection to God. When I was not studying, I spent time with my mother, learning from her. She told me that I "took to metaphysics like a fish to water." I read spiritual texts daily, whatever she recommended, mostly New Age. I meditated with her and served as her "battery" when she gave psychic readings. I cherished the morals and ethics my parents taught me. I did not smoke, drink, lie to my parents, or stay out past curfew… at least until I was eighteen, and even then, that was rare. I was ever the obedient daughter. I strove to be a good person. I was proud to save my virginity for marriage.

After my divorce, I lost my way. God was important to me, I always believed in Him, but I failed to seek that close relationship, which would have been very healing. I believed in positive thinking. My parents taught me that Satan, hell, eternal damnation, or evil in general, did not exist. I lived in a "bubble of blissful ignorance" relative to these concepts. When bad stuff happened, life would always get better. The future was bright, regardless. Only this was not the case without God. Indeed, bad things happened in the past three years, even after I was saved and studied the Bible for the first time in my life, even after teaching Sunday school for two and half years. The past few years of traumatic events were entirely my own making. I assume now they resulted from accumulated heartaches built up from everything that passed before.

One of my biggest regrets is how I left my son's father. I was so unfair to him, and it led to his misfortune as well as my own. I deprived him of having more time with his only son, who he loves more than anything or anyone else in this world to this day. I realize that it takes "two to tango," that I was unhappy for a reason, but I should have tried harder. I certainly should not have fled the state where he lived, putting a great distance between him and our son. At the time, I thought I was doing the right thing. I find it easy to second guess everything now after all these years, but if I had had a relationship with God, Jesus, and the Holy Spirit as I have now, I am convinced things would have turned out healthier.

After breaking up with my son's father, the next relationship I entered was unhealthy and negative, but I truly loved this man, Phil, and very good things came from our time together. For instance, he helped me immeasurably with the confidence required to overcome barriers to entry into a graduate study program. He supported me emotionally, mentally, and academically as I pursued a master of library science. Remember the dream I had to become a professor of Sociology? That was out the window with my divorce, which immediately followed college graduation in 1994. After that, I usually worked secretarial positions. Fast forward to 2001, I was working as an administrative assistant at East Carolina University. Employees were eligible for a part-time tuition stipend, and Phil encouraged me to take advantage of it. He was highly intelligent, earning three bachelor's degrees in four years. He tried to pursue graduate school but was burned out, so he dropped out and "went over the road" as a truck driver. Almost like the situation with my mother, he enjoyed graduate school by proxy. Whenever I failed to grasp concepts, such as complex statistical research tasks in a research methods class, he helped me comprehend them, and I aced the courses. We went on fun camping trips that my son and I enjoyed immensely. We rented movies, ate Chinese takeout, shared much humor, and delighted in intellectually stimulating conversations. Phil loved my son, helped him with his homework, and spoiled him at Christmas every year.

Unfortunately, Phil drank too much. I failed to see this in the beginning. His drinking was as severe as my stepfather's... leading to many miserable times. I agonized over exposing my son to this problem; now, he had to learn to cope with what I had to as a teenager. My stepfather was a wonderful person and human being, but when he was drunk, he was challenging, as it darkened his personality. I loved Phil deeply enough that I could not extricate myself. At least not until after I graduated with an MLS degree and moved to Texas to take my second professional librarian position at a small private college. After this move, everything fell apart spectacularly. By this point, my mother lived with us. The house we bought together was a dud; it literally disintegrated after three months post-purchase. My mother encouraged me to kick Phil out of our lives. Although he had quit drinking, he was unwilling to work and simply did nothing other than sitting in a chair watching TV, not showering or changing clothes, but wearing the same bathrobe daily. When the house fell apart, I asked him what he wanted to do to save it, and he said, "Nothing." I knew it was over then, and backed by my mother, I told him to move out.

This is so hard to contemplate now, knowing the subsequent years of homelessness he endured. As human beings, we cannot save each other, only Jesus can, but my heart still aches over my callousness. I cannot help feeling I was too hard. Years dull the memories. I am challenged to recall my misery and frustration, how defeated I felt only months after relocating, my dreams of a successful new life together in Texas flushed away. Essentially, I left broken hearts in my wake. I contemplate my life back to my first major heartbreak and the pains of childhood and teen years and wonder at my sanity. I struggle daily with negative thoughts, whether it is my conscience or the enemy's lies, depression, anxiety, stupidity, worthlessness, perpetual failure... Every time things come together, I feel on top of the world; then, they unravel stunningly, and the bubble bursts again.

---

What went down the few years prior to this writing led to the greatest faux pas of my life, the absolute worst, tragic mistakes, just when I was at the height of my career. I was saved, happily flying high in 2017. New circumstances, increasingly challenging, took their toll to the point of no return. I coped in an unhealthy way and failed miserably, resulting in the greatest loss yet. The accumulation of the negative life events contributed to my greatest downfall.

What happened truly should not have, though, given all the blessings of the past decade, for which my current husband is largely responsible. The year I found myself single in the wake of the disastrous end with Phil was 2007. I began January single and free for the first time since 2000. By the end of September, I met Tim, and it was mutual love at first sight. I was not looking for it, and neither was he. I needed two good years single to truly get to know myself again and heal from past hurts, but then and to this day, I honestly feel in my heart that God brought us together. Magic and fireworks quickly deepened into an abiding love based on friendship, caring, and respect. We experienced rough patches in the first few years. Most couples do. If any couple tells me they never had problems or arguments, I think one of them is lying. Naturally, as flawed human beings, we will disagree, argue, and most likely hurt each other at times. No one is perfect, and I beg to differ with anyone who says otherwise. Only one perfect person ever walked on earth, Jesus Christ as God incarnate.

Despite our early challenges, we surmounted all obstacles. After dating five years, we married in 2013. We are in love to this day. My love continues to deepen for him, as impossible as that seems when I think I cannot love him any more than I do now, deeply and completely. He is a good stepdad to my son. They had their contentious arguments when my son was at home as a teenager, stubborn and typically rebellious. My husband was very stern, sometimes too severe with his words, but today they are close, getting along splendidly. They love each other very much. I am grateful for the values Tim instilled in my son, whom we both are so proud that he entered the Navy and serves his country.

Several other personal losses contributed to my heartache, including three miscarriages, one with Phil, two with my husband. Tim and I suffered the loss of his best friend, who we both loved and cared for deeply. He was a very sweet person who committed suicide a few years ago. We suffered the untimely death of my father-in-law. Losing my mother was a blow. I lost friends and a nephew when they were young, well before their time, but most people experience such grief in life.

---

What led to my most recent, "spectacular" downfall? The college that employed me as an academic librarian was a pleasant place to work, where I was happy. The job was peaceful, cushy, supportive of my work, my effort to build a career and a reputation as one in service to the profession, and travel to conferences for presenting talks on panels and workshops. That is until the boss who hired me, who held me in high regard, decided to retire. Things went downhill after his departure, and although it took about five or six months, the "writing on the wall" became clear when the new director did not regard me well. Eventually, it became evident to me that I had to leave. The new boss and I were incompatible, and it seemed there was nothing I could do or say to change that. I realized if I did not leave, things would become unbearable for me. By mid-2017, a new position opened up nearby, and after soul searching, I decided to explore the opportunity, which I accepted when it was offered to me.

At first, the change worked out quite well. I was nervous, anxious, changing from one type of librarianship into another one new to me, where I lacked experience, creating a steep learning curve. In the beginning of 2017, I committed myself to serving God and felt the Holy Spirit guide me. I prayed hard every day and received the divine help I needed. Every day giving glory to God, I performed my duties successfully. I dove in, taught myself, and excelled. The patrons loved me, and so did my colleagues. Everyone was well pleased, and I was so happy. I was happy at church also, having the fulfilling opportunity to teach Sunday school, where I was truly the student learning from them, but they generally loved the way I taught and said God gifted me with teaching ability. I agreed with them; God called me to it and gave me what I needed in that endeavor.

Before long, however, stressors emerged at work and in my personal life. A few months passed happily on the new job, from August through October. Then in November, a patron began coming in daily, staying all day long. No one warned me about her, and I did not know what I was in for with her. I did not realize how continuous her presence would be. I could tell from the beginning she was very needy but failed to see how ongoing her neediness would be and how demanding she would become, so I made the mistake at the outset of doing more for her than I should have. I thought with the first few favors, that would be it, and she would move on. I was so wrong. I learned the hard way to set boundaries from the beginning with each patron, but with this lady in particular, that hardly would have made a difference. I learned after the fact that she had been a "pest" to the entire community for years, particularly for my predecessor, who set the precedent for demanding patrons by doing everything asked of her, so that extra help was naturally expected to continue with me.

Soon, this patron prayed over my desk for up to an hour and would have continued for hours if I didn't stop her. Her expectations were excessive, and soon, she exhausted me. When I began resisting her, she harassed me. I felt dread as soon as I saw her heading into the library. By the end of January, I could see how poorly I handled the situation from the start, allowing her to harass other patrons. I realized that they were not returning. I had to stop her antics. I searched for best practices in rule posting and enforcement, hoping this would help the situation by establishing boundaries for all patrons. Deep down, I knew this would have no effect on her.

Eventually, she was banned from the entire courthouse. As it turned out, she cornered many people, workers and visitors alike, across all departments. This happened after a year of dealing with her daily with only a few brief breaks when she disappeared for a few weeks, only to return. Over that year, the situation became so stressful, and I coped poorly. I began drinking every night after work just to relax.

After my breakup with Phil, I drank again for the first time after five years of abstinence. When I was with him, I detested drinking because of his severe alcoholism. When I found myself single again, I felt free to drink socially. At times during the ensuing ten years, I drank too much, after which I quit for several months up to a year. I could foresee my proclivity developing into a problem. I should have sought counseling to deal with all life's heartaches. Perhaps mental health care could have helped me avoid such a costly crescendo.

I quit drinking early in 2017 in preparation for "the sleeve" surgery, which reduces the stomach size. I was morbidly obese, having several comorbidities, including prediabetes and very high total cholesterol levels, which qualified me full coverage of the surgery's cost under my health insurance. I "jumped through many hoops," including a diagnosis of sleep apnea. I passed all requirements for surgery, which was scheduled for July 2017. When I first sought the surgery, I did not know how soon I would change jobs. Luckily, I was able to get the surgery while still employed at the college. Unfortunately, I had to change jobs quickly thereafter. I recovered at home only a few days and squeezed in a long road trip to see my son graduate boot camp, returned to work for one more week, and then went directly to my new job.

Subsequently, I lost excess weight quickly, shrinking a dress size each month… eighteen, seventeen, sixteen, fourteen, twelve, ten, and finally a size eight by February 2018. The surgery is an important consideration relative to my renewed drinking. When I picked up the bottle again, I was not thinking rationally, not clear-headed enough to remember that there is an important reason consuming alcohol is strongly discouraged for bariatric patients. Having a tiny stomach or lacking one in the case of gastric bypasses, the body cannot process alcohol, which strongly hits the bloodstream. When I learned this, I remembered Phil had a gastric bypass in the 1990s. His alcoholism, with its effect on him, made new sense to me. I never took illegal drugs, but some likened the effect of alcohol in such circumstances to the effect of crack or cocaine. The high is instantaneous, intense, and very addictive. Later, I researched the effects of drinking in bariatric patients and learned it is becoming a more well-known and documented problem. Many bariatric patients never had alcohol problems until after surgery, and the ramifications are quite serious for these patients, somewhere around ten percent of people with this type of surgery.[1]

Drinking again was the last thing I should have done, and it became a serious problem quickly. Soon I was drinking every day, and this is what led to my spectacular downfall. Other stressors on the home front contributed to my struggles. I blame no one else, but the patron lady and the other problems served as triggers. My mental health declined. I experienced a mental/nervous/emotional breakdown. Oddly, outside of difficult people and challenges in my life, I was, contrarily, very happy with most aspects of my new job and with my church, particularly with teaching Sunday school. Nevertheless, when I began drinking again, I couldn't stop no matter how hard I tried. I begged and pleaded with God, Jesus, the Holy Spirit. I literally prostrated myself on the floor in heartfelt, prayerful supplication, "Please, please take this from me. Just take it!" I heard other Christians pray this way and testify it worked from callers to Christian radio shows. Boom! Just like that, they were completely healed, the desire left them, Jesus removed their defects, addictions, and they never touched a drop again, or a drug or a cigarette, whatever the problem. I thought the same would be true for me. When the situation persisted, I questioned whether I was truly saved. Had I just imagined it?

Conversely, many miracles took place in 2017. Everything lined up perfectly, new jobs for myself and others, the surgery, losing all the extra weight... The love and compassion God placed in my heart. I experienced pure joy in helping others. I was gratified God saved me from myself in so many ways, just for choosing me... No, I am absolutely convinced God chose me and has plans for me. This book is part of His plans. The main point of this writing is to give Christian testimony, glorify Him, and help others with encouragement and inspiration to find Christ and be healed. Maybe my story will also help others avoid my costly mistakes. Why I had to take this difficult path, only God knows. When I landed the law librarian job, I thought it was my new purpose until retirement, helping and serving the poor people who accessed the library's services, people who could not afford lawyers or needed other types of legal help. Apparently not, though, since after only eighteen months, the best job of my life, with its health benefits, retirement, and life savings, and any shred of dignity and pride I had left, was lost. This book is about following Jesus into jail... for having an alcohol problem escalate to the point that I had to serve time through incarceration upon two DWI convictions.

The following is an account of how that came about, what happened before, during, and after I served my sentence, and how the Holy Spirit directed me to turn my mistakes into helping others find Jesus. I am to give God all the glory by shining His light into dark places, showing His love, bringing others hope through His healing power, love, forgiveness, and redemption. He directs me to continue to serve Him, discover His true purpose for my life and realign it according to His will.

# CHAPTER 1

# Monday, May 20th

## DAY 4: JAILED

God is clearly speaking to me. I am definitely meant to be here. Mutual testimony convinces me. One inmate gave me a book of daily devotions, *Living the Message* by Eugene Peterson.[2] I was locked up Friday, May 17th, the day my judge sentenced me to almost a year in county jail, 335 days. The May 17th message in Peterson's book is about Jonah and the whale. God confined Jonah to the belly of the whale while he was fleeing from Him. God had work for Jonah to do, so He stopped him in his tracks, restricting his movements; Jonah had no choice but to be still and listen.[3]

I am a hundred percent sure God has work for me to do, and he stopped me for multiple reasons. First, He saved me from myself. I was in a downward spiral, from which I could not save myself. I tried to give it to God. I begged Him to take it from me. He did not respond. From this, I understood that He was not going to answer my prayer because it was not His Will. He has other plans for me. He knew I would not voluntarily leave my job. He used my addiction to catch me and put me in the belly of *my* whale. This evening I read the May 17th entry about Jonah and the whale.

Upon sentencing, I was "booked in" (i.e., processed into incarceration) at the local county jail. Opportunities to testify or at least to pray for other women began immediately in the holding tank, which precedes assignment to a tank in the "general population," which refers to inmates in regular tanks, who are not trustees or in isolation, etc. The first lady I met was mentally disturbed. She gave me the impression of being possessed. She spoke in different voices and nonsensical narratives, mostly dark stuff. "So you think *they* are dead, but I'm bringing *them* back to life, and they are going to kick your butt!" Admittedly, she used harsher language, which I will not repeat here. I immediately prayed for her, "God, please bind her demons and cast them out. Bind them as they are in heaven.[4] Bring peace to this poor soul who is being so tormented." At one point, she looked directly at me and, crying, asked, "Are we okay?" to which I simply replied, "Yes." She nodded and remained silent for a bit before her litany resumed.

After a while, she asked me, "Are you a teacher?" I was amazed by her perception in a moment of lucidity. I affirmed that I was, in the form of a librarian. I wondered if she was both insane and possessed. After some time, I stretched my muscles out of boredom. Naturally, I felt stressed, and I figured stretching would help alleviate soreness, pain, stiffness, and release of oxytocin.[5]

My companion commented, "Well, look at you, Miss Yoga Librarian." In the two hours that I spent with her, she had brief moments of lucidity. When I said that I was thirsty, she pointed out which cup was probably the cleanest from those left behind, and I decided to take my chances, washing it out as best as possible in order to get water from the tap above the toilet.

I asked her, "Are you from Greenville?"

"No, I'm from New York. I miss my husband."

"Where is he?"

She only responded with an incomprehensible string of phrases and profanities. Sometimes she sounded like she was quoting movies, "You want to make a deal? I'll make you a deal. Me and my guys will get shovels and clobber you. How does that sound?" Realizing questions only led to more rambling, I resolved to just keep praying for her rather than attempt conversation.

A few hours later, the CO (correction officer) called her out of the holding tank. About half an hour later, she tapped on the window and said, "She's not coming back. I warned you she is certifiable, didn't I?" I gave her the thumbs-up sign. A short time later, a young woman I will call Samantha was brought in. I asked what she was in for, and she answered, "Revocation of probation." She appeared completely sober, but after observing her restless pace into the late hours, I wondered if she was coming down from drug use. She told me she had not slept in days. She struck me as intelligent and well-spoken. She conversed on a level that belied being well-educated. We talked about our jobs, family, and experiences stemming from our legal problems. When it seemed appropriate, I shared with her how only my faith in God was helping me through my literal and figurative tribulations, overcoming the stress and anxiety of losing my legal fight to avoid incarceration. She agreed that faith in God is necessary and said that she was saved but recently had not been leaning on Him. She related in a mature way with me as we talked until the next young woman arrived. Mid-speech, Samantha looked up and said, "Oh no, this looks like a tough one."

I followed her gaze and saw an attractive, youthful woman with long, black hair and a tattoo-covered body. She sat as far away as possible from us, seemingly antisocial. However, Samantha was outgoing and soon drew her into conversation, which ensued for hours. Samantha's transformation in character and speech in order to relate to a tough girl from the "hood" amazed me.

"Man, I can't wait to get out of the [*expletive*] joint and back to the hood," declared Amber (my name for her). Samantha communicated perfectly with Amber. Their conversation flowed in lingo appropriate for "jail talk," as Samantha termed it when I whispered to her that I could not follow much of their conversation. I reminded myself of Will Ferrell's character in the movie *Get Hard*, which would be the case frequently over the next few months.

Since I was unable to participate in their dialog, I just prayed over them. I never felt led to testify to Amber, but I expressed my sympathy and gave her positive affirmations. For instance, she said, "I've gotten so fat! You should have seen how *hot* I was before jail. Eight months have put so much weight on me!" Amber had been transported in from another jail.

"No!" Samantha and I exclaimed simultaneously. "You are beautiful regardless!" I added.

However, Amber's hurting soul shone through. During the next twenty hours together in holding, she began flirting with a male inmate in the next holding tank. They shouted at each other through a crack in the wall. She had a high-pitched, piercing voice. By one o'clock in the morning, I had a splitting headache. In the meantime, Samantha joined in, greatly upsetting Amber. Subsequently, they argued with each other, and Amber screamed at Mr. Flirt next door for responding to Samantha. By flirtations, I mean that explicit sexual acts were described in detail. Amber figured out how to see Mr. Flirt's reflection in the opposite door's window. She instructed him on how to see her as well for the purpose of flashing him. Apparently, they were successful, judging by his approving vocal responses, but I closed my eyes, not wanting to see this desperate act of a hurting twenty-year-old woman needing love and acceptance. With my migraine, I knew this was not the time to talk to her.

At around 2 a.m. Saturday, a third woman, Kristy, arrived. She simply said, "I'm very high," curled up on the floor, promptly fell asleep, impervious to the hollering. In Sunday's early morning hours, I gave up my patience and begged Samantha and Amber to please be quiet and let me sleep. They sat down for a few minutes and then quickly resumed screaming. I was miserable. Suddenly the door burst open, and a CO entered, yelling at the two. He had previously been on Amber's case twice. This time he really made his point clear, threatening solitary in the observational room across from the intake desk.

He added, "Can't you see this nice lady is trying to sleep?" I doubt that my lack of sleep concerned them, but they finally became quiet, allowing me a blissful break from the constant stream of profanity and sexually explicit talk. As my head throbbed, I prayed, "God, please bless them, shower them with love, comfort, and prick their hearts with Your Holy Spirit." I hoped I did not fail God by lacking the courage to speak up more. I just sensed it would not go over well.

We did not get out of the tank until I spent thirty hours in it. This time was rough. In holding, one must sit and sleep on a concrete bench or floor. In spring and summer, blankets are not issued, and the holding tank was freezing. Kristy awoke, shivering, and buzzed intake to ask for a blanket. The responding guard replied, "No, ma'am. We do not hand out blankets in the summertime."

"But the last time I was here, we were given blankets. Please, it's freezing!" We were all desperate for warmth, hugging our bodies under our jail uniform issued shirts. I thought, *Good for her being brave enough to ask.*

"The rules have changed," the CO replied. "Blankets only in winter. I am *not* breaking the rule for you!" I could not blame the guard; it would not be worth being fired over. But still… my body was covered in bruises from tossing and turning on cold concrete. My bones ached. The guards had to harden their hearts. *I could not do that job,* I thought. The lights are also kept on in holding, twenty-four seven.

Being sent to the back was a relief, as scary as the prospect was that I could be put in a tank with tough, rough, mean women. I need not have worried. I was "classified" with others who had probation revoked for similar offenses, including DWIs, drug possession, and petty theft. I was issued a green wristband, standing for "no threat." Some of the women in my assigned tank had green wristbands, and others had orange (moderate threat), but no one in our tank had a red one. The CO who processed me into the general population told me that she was putting me in the tank with the "nicest ladies" because she could tell I was "nice." She encouraged me to apply for trustee, or inmate worker, where some work half of their sentence off, and I did so. Humorously, I said, "I'd like that; I'm smart!"

"I can tell," she replied. Remembering this makes me giggle. What an inane thing to say.

The moment I walked into my assigned tank, the women stopped what they were doing, looked up, smiled, and greeted me warmly. They immediately assisted me with getting situated, covering my mattress (a plastic thing with a built-in "pillow") with what looked like a giant pillowcase. Later one of the sweetest girls, for whom I will use the pseudonym Penina, or Peni for short, told me that as soon as I walked in the room, I brought peace with me. She "felt my energy" and knew immediately she liked me and thought that I would be good for her. That touched me deeply.

Another woman, who I call Bahati, smiled warmly at me and waved me over to her bunk, pointing to the one below her, against the wall in the corner of the room. That spot appealed to me. After selecting it, the dynamics of the room emerged. Bahati seemed friendly and warm. She reminded me of an African tribal woman by the way she fashioned her jail-issued shirt as a turban. The three other women include one who looks thirty; some may describe as a "butch." I shall call her Alex. Another one, approximately thirty, Hispanic, and I choose the pseudonym Loreana for her. Peni is very young, around twenty, with exotic, tropical looks (hence pseudonym Penani).

Peni drew me aside and whispered in my ear, "We think you may want to consider changing bunks because Bahati will take your stuff. Move over one bunk and put your basket on the other side of the bed away from her." I just nodded in surprise as they moved my stuff for me over one bunk. I wondered if this was true or prejudice? I decided to keep an open mind and not judge the situation, asking God to reveal the truth to me. My first instinct was to protect Bahati because she is African American.

Dinner arrived shortly, and as we sat down to eat, I noticed that Bahati took her tray to her bunk. I thought, *She's being excluded.* I sat with the other three at one of the two tables. I could not eat much, trying only a little of what I thought was meat, but later discovered that most of the "meat" is soy, which tastes horrible. Being a bariatric patient, I could not eat most of the tray food because of carbohydrates. My diet should consist of protein and vitamins mainly. I took two bites of vegetables, also tasting intolerable. I offered my tray to my three table-mates, who cleared it with amazing speed into other receptacles. They had a tall stack of cornbread and cake. Bahati hopped off her bunk, saying, "I'll take some bread!" but the other three chorused, "No!" I was shocked and surprised! I thought, *This is not right!* Jesus said if someone asks for something, give it without regret or expectation of reimbursement.[6] I said nothing but determined in the future, my tray would be shared equally.

I had entered jail at 11 a.m. Friday, May 17th, and arrived in the general population at 6 p.m. Saturday evening, exhausted from the thirty hours in holding. Suffice it to say, I was too exhausted after dinner to accept invitations to play cards or read the other women's books. They were so warm, welcoming, and hospitable to me. I wish they had the same regard for Bahati as well, but I would soon see why the women were acting as they were toward her. At any rate, I politely declined social invitations, took a shower to get the "ick" off from holding (a place of pee stains and vomit-covered walls). After that, I collapsed in my bunk, grateful for a mattress, albeit very thin. At this point, I was not going to complain. Rather, I fell into a deep sleep.

---

The next day, Sunday, was peaceful overall, although the noise level remained high. Alex is quiet-spoken, while Loreana and Peni speak loudly. Peni screams through the wall, flirting with a male inmate next door. I thought, *Oh no, not this again.* She is also passing notes to him through a crack in the wall's corner. I was tired, sleepy and my head was splitting with a screaming migraine, making my mood bad. Yet I continuously prayed, speaking words of peace over the ladies. I drifted in and out of sleep whenever I could tune out the noise.

Alex "ruled the roost" with an iron fist as the day unwrapped, further revealing the same tank dynamics. She controls the TV, keeping it on the programming she prefers. Once, when Bahati thought Alex was asleep, she attempted to change the channel, but Alex said firmly and authoritatively, "I am watching that!"

"Sorry!" Bahati exclaimed, retreating to her bunk, hiding under her blanket.

Breakfast is served at 6:30 a.m. Immediately upon receiving my tray, I walked to Bahati's bunk, offering her my bread. She joyfully accepted. I turned and saw the other women's expressions as they stared at me, silently questioning, *Why did you do that?*

"I share equally," I announced. They exchanged looks. I could barely eat anything. I recognized the "sausage" for what it was: soy. Looking dismal, tasting disgusting, I took one bite and regretted it. I took two bites of fruit salad and passed my tray to the ladies.

"Is that all you are eating?" They exclaimed.

"Yes."

"Why?"

"I'm a bariatric patient."

"What?"

"I had a stomach surgery called 'the sleeve,' which reduces your stomach size up to seventy-five percent.[7] I can't eat much, and I'm not allowed to eat carbs, which break down to sugar in the bloodstream." Loreana asked me to clarify what I meant by "carbs."

"Carbohydrates, such as potatoes, rice, pasta, bread, any grain product, break down into sugar, which is the greatest offender in weight gain[8] and are difficult for the tiny stomach to digest. According to my bariatric surgeon, my diet must consist of protein and vitamins."

"Oh, so you can't eat any of this?" Loreana asked. I shook my head.

"So y'all will be enjoying extra portions," I said in my best southern drawl, grinning. They smiled back. I glanced over my shoulder at Bahati, who was looking at me, and we smiled at each other.

The ladies break food into pieces and mix it together, scraping it off the trays into plastic containers, adding flavoring such as hot sauce, cheese, etc., and eating until full. Then they cover their bowl with lids to eat the rest later. Leftovers never go to waste. As I watched the amount they consumed, I thought about how I could eat like that once upon a time. About seven years previously, I was at an all-time high of 210 pounds, which was quite a bit on my small five-foot-one frame. Fat has always shown on my face first. I hated the way my face looked when I was that fat and how I was constantly biting the insides of my cheeks and my tongue. I could eat two whole pizzas. I sat there in my musings, grateful I could not eat like that now but worried about what I would eat during my stay. On the other hand, if I should become skinny, I would be delighted. I am about twenty pounds away from my goal of 130 pounds. I recently put ten pounds back on, contributed greatly by consuming wine, doubtlessly. I realize these women are comforting themselves as I had once done, obviously due to stressful incarceration and perhaps by past traumas.

Shortly after breakfast, the CO duty banged on our window and called, "Rec!"

"Rec?" I asked.

"Recreation," they explained. "We get it twice a week for one hour each time."

"Is that all?" I queried, appalled. I imagined that we would get at least one hour a day, save for inclement weather.

"Yes," they confirmed.

I was amazed. Two hours a week total for sunshine and fresh air. The movies never seemed to portray this.[9]

The "rec" yard (as painted on the door going out to it) is relatively small, but it's difficult for me to say how many feet or yards by width, length, and height since I am not a good judge of distance. The walls are extremely high and bordered with barbed and razor wire. Heavy-duty fencing covers the top. All one can see are cotton ball clouds gently drifting across a small patch of blue sky. This is better than nothing, and I thank God for the opportunity to breathe fresh air.

In the yard, I spoke with Bahati. She was relaxed and friendly. I liked her. Well, I liked all the ladies being so sweet to me. Bahati informed me that although she was a "Christian," she was also "clairvoyant."

"I see spirits," she said.

"Do you see them all the time?"

"No."

"Do you see any now?"

"No, but I have at times in jail. I always see them over my bong."

I guessed she probably did harder drugs than marijuana.

"I'm homeless because our house burnt down. My mother blamed me, but I didn't do it."

She went on to describe her clairvoyance, which began when she was a child.

"The first three years of my life, I did not talk. My father took me to a school for learning disabilities. But I wasn't retarded. I'm here for drugs causing the revocation of probation."

"I'm here for revocation of my probation, which was revoked for DWI 2," I offered.

"People don't understand the psychic thing. Seeing spirits," she replied.

"I understand it because my mother did. But I wouldn't tell everyone this if I were you. They'll think you are crazy."

At this point, Loreana and Peni called me over. I noticed that Bahati walked on (the inmates walk in a circle until tiring; then they sit on the concrete ground). The two women were sitting side by side, so I squatted next to them to hear them better. "What is she doing?" Loreana asked, and I glanced over my shoulder to see Bahati standing still, nodding her head, eyes closed, wringing her hands. "You know she's crazy, right?" Loreana asked me.

"Really?" I replied. I began to believe it.

"Yes," they both replied.

"You have to be careful, Shannon," Peni informed me. "She will steal from you."

"We hear our baskets move in the night and wake up to find her snooping through them," added Loreana. "She attacked me once also."

"In here?" I asked.

"No, before, on the outside. Back when I did dope. We were both on it. She scratched my arm, made it bleed."

"She has a temper in here too," added Peni. "You will see it. She screams and shouts profanities."

"Wow," I responded, feeling surprised. "Thanks for the warning."

"You're welcome," Loreana answered. "We like you, Shannon. We are watching for you."

"Well, thank you, ladies. I like you too."

"So why are you here?" Loreana asked.

"I broke my probation by getting a second DWI."

"How much time did they give you?"

"A year."

"Wow, what were you on probation for?"

"DWI 1."

"What exactly happened when you broke probation?" Loreana continued.

"I was really stupid. My husband wanted me to go to the store on a Sunday morning. I should have been at church, but I was having a bad weekend. Stress at home. Not from my husband. We have a wonderful, strong marriage. He loves me so much. He is so good to me. He stands by me. I do feel like his family stays upset with me. It's hard. I feel so much pressure. I was very tired. I told my husband that I didn't want to go. I stayed home from church because I needed to rest. I worked eight hours of community service on Saturday on top of my forty-hour work week and ten-hour commute time... anyway, I was just exhausted and on the edge of an emotional breakdown. I still can't make sense of it, though. It was pure madness because I had already been drinking that morning. My husband couldn't tell, though, amazingly, and he just directed me to go to the nearest store to get him cracked black pepper. Unfortunately, I decided to head to Greenville to buy some wine. I went to Walmart after stopping by a convenience store for the wine. I was drinking in the car. When I pulled up in the parking lot, I parked nose to nose with another lady on the garden side of the store and apparently tapped her car with mine. I got out to head into the store, but she hopped out of her car and stopped me and said I hit her car. I looked at her bumper and mine. There was no damage, and I said so, asking, 'So what is the problem?' 'Well, I am calling the police!' she exclaimed. She got back into her car, and I saw her gesticulating wildly as she spoke on the phone. I got back into my car and inexplicably just sat there and waited. It's all a bit hazy. When the police arrived, they questioned me, conducted a field sobriety test, and arrested me."

"They immediately arrested you right there in the Walmart parking lot?" asked Loreana.

"Yes."

"They could tell you had been drinking?"

"Oh yes. From the sobriety test, it was obvious. I probably smelled of it too."

Peni jumped into the conversation to narrate her story. We were all classified together for "Motions to Revoke Probation." She described similar circumstances, getting caught with drugs. She detailed past traumas, including her parents pimping her out and being raped. Her traumas greatly surmounted mine. I studied her face and surmised that her bright, energetic spirit and upbeat attitude covered deep pain, but I thought, *She is strong, and she is going to survive this and do something important with her life.* I said as much to her.

"God definitely has a plan for me, but I need to get straight and heal," she responded.

"Amen!" I replied.

"Rec" was over then, and we returned to our tank.

That afternoon, I spoke with Alex. Her bunk is next to mine. Bahati was on her bunk, up to my right, wrapped tightly in her blanket. I could only see her shape but could tell she was facing away. Peni is on Alex's left; she was sleeping on her mattress on the floor between Alex and Loreana. The second installment of *Twilight* played on FX.

Alex and I discussed our faith. "I can tell you are a Christian, a true follower of Christ," she said. "You have a sweet, kind, generous spirit. I am like that too. The first few weeks I was here, I enjoyed sharing my food with the others. But you have to be careful, especially with Bahati. If you share once with her, she will expect it constantly, and you will run out of supplies quickly. She's indigent and cannot make a contribution. So it is all take and no give. I am relying on my family's support, especially my mother's. I quickly ran through a lot of money she put on my account. She got mad at me because I asked her for more. I told her why, and she explained to me that it wasn't fair to her that she puts her hard-earned money in her daughter's account, trying to help her, only to have half the stuff given away. She's right, you know? So I could no longer share. The next time I made coffee, I had to tell Bahati no, and she became very angry and cussed at me. There's another side to her you haven't seen yet. We all have," Alex said, indicating herself, Peni, and Loreana, "and we've submitted multiple requests to have her moved, but they fall on deaf ears. They're not going to do anything. And she steals. My cards ended up in her basket. She will go through yours if she thinks no one is looking. Keep it covered up and between our beds. I'm watching out for you."

This was much to digest. I thought about how Jesus instructed us to give freely what we are asked for, without expectation of recompense, and if anyone steals from us, offer them the rest as well.[10] Alex is right, though, to honor her mother by obeying her on how to use the funds bestowed upon her. I realized, naively, how challenging it can be at times to strictly adhere to Jesus' instruction. I would find this problematic throughout my incarceration.

Alex continued to share with me her growth and insights recently gained by reading Christian literature she borrowed from the jail's library. She recommended reading certain books such as *Unqualified*.[11] Peni jumped up upon hearing this and enthusiastically ran over to me with a book she borrowed, *Sold to the Highest Bidder*,[12] insisting I read it right away. "It's very good!"

Alex also gave me her copy of *Living The Message*[13] and a free daily devotional, *Our Daily Bread*.[14] We testified to each other, Alex sharing with me how Jesus was changing her life positively, and I responded with many, "Yes!" and "Me too!"

Late in the afternoon, Alex was called for a visit. I hoped my husband would come. I knew he was dropping by to put a little cash in my account so I could purchase some needed commissary items, executed through the telephone system. I was never called for a visit that day. Later Tim told me a CO in the lobby told him that I had to serve a week before I was allowed visitors.

While Alex was gone, Loreana switched the TV channel, settling for the movie *Shrek*. "Thank God! I'm sick of watching the *Twilight* movies over and over! You know Alex controls the TV, right? We don't get to watch our cartoons! She always has the sound blasting too!" she exclaimed.

"I like to watch the news," Bahati contributed, sitting up, gaining interest in her surroundings with the temporary absence of Alex. "But nope, no news!"

Loreana continued, "You realize she's a tank bully, right? She orders us around, and she doesn't allow Bahati to do anything, even play cards with us…" She glanced over at Bahati, a sudden comrade in the case against Alex.

"Geez," I replied, "that ain't right!" I felt torn. I already cared about each of these women. A definite rift existed between Alex and Bahati; however, I could see both sides. *God*, I thought, *You are giving me so many opportunities to testify, to learn, and to pray for others. Thank You, Father!*

---

This Monday morning began normally. I am settling in comfortably. When I received my lunch tray, I sat down at the table with the clique, not thinking to offer Bahati something first that I couldn't eat. I was sizing up my tray, deciding what I would and would not eat. I could get away with just eating a few bites of vegetables. Bahati sat at the table next to us and asked, "Shannon, do you want my vegetables?"

"No, thank you," I replied, realizing I had more than I could eat.

"Bahati! Let her eat first before asking for her food!" Alex commanded.

Oh boy! Did the fireworks begin! Bahati immediately jumped to her feet while a tirade of foul expletives emitted from her mouth, including gay slurs. Appalled, I said, "It's okay! It's okay!"

"I know it's okay, Shannon!" Bahati replied and continued her assault on Alex. She didn't strike out with fists, but she used her physical presence to intimidate Alex, leaning over her. Alex replied with something drowned out by Bahati's escalating volume.

While Alex went over to the buzzer, I abandoned my tray and lay on my bunk, feeling miserable. Bahati's explosive tirade sounded like Satan himself, calling Alex a "hypocrite who worships false gods," and so forth. More words flew at Alex than I ever dare to write here. Bahati frightened me at first, but then I became increasingly angry. However, I recognize Alex had been bullying Bahati for weeks. The fight calmed down when the CO arrived, who first called Alex out into the vestibule and out of earshot. I was determined to keep an open mind.

Next, Bahati was called out. She returned, and everyone was tensely silent. An hour passed, and the COs called me out into the vestibule. With the rest unable to hear, the first CO began questioning me.

"Did Bahati try to take your tray even before you began eating?" questioned the first CO, Ms. Hughes.

"No," I answered honestly. Mrs. Hughes turned to Ms. Randolph and said, "I told you she was lying." *Uh-oh*, I thought.

"Did Bahati ask you for food before you finished eating?" asked Ms. Hughes.

"No," I answered again, honestly. "She offered me her vegetables, which I declined. We had been trading items before that."

"That is what inmates normally do," acknowledged Mrs. Hughes. I nodded. "So what actually happened?" she asked.

"Well, after I declined the food, Alex told Bahati to leave me alone and let me eat."

"Would you say Alex is a 'bully'?" asked Mrs. Hughes.

"She bullies Bahati and controls the room, the TV, and orders the others around, from what they tell me," I answered. I was honestly frank with her. That was my assessment. However, I had just seen something frightening in Bahati, so I added, "Bahati got really mad and yelled profanities at Alex, intimidating her by leaning over her. I saw what the others say they see in Bahati." At that, the COs nodded. "I was frightened," I added.

"I think Bahati might be crazy." With that, the COs exchanged a second and told me to go back inside. I hoped I conveyed a balanced and unbiased account from what I observed.

I returned to my bunk, focusing on another run of *Twilight*, the TV back on FX with Alex's return. Alex laid calmly on her bunk, with Peni and Loreana chatting on her other side. Bahati was wrapped like a cocoon again in her blanket on her bunk.

After a few hours, Mrs. Hughes returned with Ms. Randolph, the mechanical door unlocking announcing their arrival, and called Alex by last name, stating, "Get packed up now! We are moving you!"

I was shocked and immediately regretful. I hoped Bahati would be moved because of the other's accounts of previous incidents, after which they each submitted multiple requests to have her moved. All testimonials of Bahati's behavior seemed to be ignored. Perhaps jail staff waited for physical violence as justification before moving Bahati to what would probably be a more secure area or perhaps solitary confinement. Bahati fought against this possibility fiercely. She told me she spent several weeks in the holding tank, insisting that she couldn't be in solitary confinement because she had been raped in solitary in the past and feared it happening again.

I was sad to see Alex go because we bonded over shared testimonials, have similar problems, and shared recommendations on reading material. Also, she is calm, quiet, and, other than having a control issue, is polite and respectful.

Peni and Loreana voiced their protests immediately. Alex said, "If you don't like their decision, tell them!" They ran to the window, banged on it, as was the procedure to catch the CO's attention.

"I don't want you to go!" wailed Peni. Then Peni and Loreana drifted back to their bunks within minutes, apparently resigned. I wanted to make a stronger case for a different outcome, so I also banged on the window but was ignored.

Meanwhile, Alex packed up her gear, unmade her bed, folded her sheet and blanket on top of her stuff, and was ready to go. Mrs. Hughes returned and said, "Let's go [Alex's last name]!"

I observed Loreana and Peni just standing there, saying nothing. Usually, Peni wouldn't hesitate to protest to the COs, as she readily had done over other issues. Puzzled, I held my peace. Just like that, Alex was gone.

Within a minute of her departure, Bahati jumped down from her bunk, delightedly changing the TV channel. I was disappointed by this because the third installment of *Twilight* was just beginning, which I had not seen in a while. I dared not protest, though, because I didn't want Bahati to blow up at me like she had Alex.

"Thank God!" exclaimed Loreana. "I was sick of *Twilight*!"

"I was sick of being ordered around!" chimed in Peni.

Once again, I was thoroughly caught off guard, left in total surprise.

"Yes!" exclaimed Loreana. "We could never watch the programming we wanted. The TV is supposed to be shared in four-hour blocks of time. She hogged the TV all day!"

"You mean you are happy now she is gone?" I asked incredulously.

"Yes!" agreed Loreana. "We like our cartoons! She refused us! She wouldn't allow us to watch the programming we wanted."

"What cartoons do you like?" I asked, my mind reeling.

"Family Guy!" they exclaimed. I realized it was Monday and asked, "You mean reruns?"

"Yes!" they both exclaimed. "We like our cartoons!" Peni reiterated. "She refuses to let us watch them!"

The two continued to discuss what they didn't like about Alex. As Bahati fiddled with the TV, I realized that one day would not be like the next.

However, this evening the four of us played many rounds of UNO. During this time, everyone seemed content.

# CHAPTER 2

# Tuesday, May 21st

## DAY 5: CHANGES

Tuesday is commissary day when items ordered by the deadline on Sunday are delivered. I ordered a few basic items, including some things that did not arrive, unfortunately, such as multivitamins. I desperately need them since I am unable to eat most of the tray food. Neither did the four-inch toothbrush show up. Using the issued one-inch toothbrush is awkward. (I eventually learned that the four-inch toothbrush was disallowed, but for some reason, such items were included on our commissary list as "available" for purchase. I wonder why the county's jail commissary list is not customized appropriately.)

I received summer sausage, beef and cheese sticks, picante sauce to add flavor to the horrible food, stamps (frustratingly, I forgot to order envelopes), a note pad (on which I begin this book), earplugs, washcloth, towel, panties, boxers, deodorant, shampoo, and an extra pen. I am delighted to receive these essential items I normally could not imagine living without (but already have for a few days).

Peni ordered coffee, and she apparently borrowed a stamped envelope from Bahati with the promise of four scoops of coffee as repayment. Peni gave Bahati three scoops.

"That's half the coffee I received," explained Peni.

"Give me another scoop. You promised four," answered Bahati.

"I know, I planned to," answered Peni, "but I only received one bag of coffee instead of the two I ordered, so I don't have enough. Three scoops are half this bag. If I give you another scoop, I will have very little left."

"I don't care how little you have left, you agreed, four scoops!" demanded Bahati.

Loreana inserted herself into their argument, "Oh, for God's sake, Bahati, let her be! She can only give you three now. She will give you another one from her next order. You have enough for now!"

And bam! Just like that, we got our second volcanic explosion, the most foul, explicit language emitting from Bahati's mouth, streaming forth in an insulting tirade, now directed at Loreana. Bahati used the same physical intimidation technique, getting in Loreana's face, threatening her, using Hispanic slurs this time.

*Oh no!* I felt it boiling up in me, a molten lava flow of anger. I hate losing my temper, which is the most uncomfortable feeling because I do not wish to be this way. I am peaceful, loving, compassionate, more so for what Jesus has given me. I am non-confrontational. When my anger surfaces, I walk away or run, if I can, fearing the terrible words that may come out of my mouth. Words once said can never be retracted and may cause incredible damage or great pain. The tongue is one of the devil's greatest weapons.[15]

In response, I immediately went to the wall and buzzed the front desk at booking, having learned that banging on the window to draw the CO's attention often fails.

"Yes?" came the response.

"There's a terrible fight in here. The same person as yesterday yelling and cussing!"

"Okay," was the reply.

They never came. I imagined them at their desk, laughing, "A verbal fight! What a catastrophe!"

Eventually, the fight died off, and, fuming, I returned to my bunk and just stared up at the underside of the bunk above. I shook, my heart pounding hard.

I knew there was no reasoning with Bahati. She was just like the craziest person I had ever had to deal with in the public library I'd run solo before coming to jail. She had the same modus operandi and desire to steal.

The "crazy horse lady" grabbed handfuls of free stuff I put out for the public's convenience, such as paper and binder clips, that I purchased out of pocket every time she came in. The "crazy horse lady" was a total mental case, but she had excellent acting skills, was highly intelligent, and extremely manipulative. I did not catch onto her game quickly. At first, she acted all nice, sweet, and soft, portraying herself as a victim of almost everyone in the community.

Bahati reminded me so much of her, and from this experience, I knew I could not reason with her. Therefore, I thought, *She has to go before she drives me crazy, just like "crazy horse lady."* There were more than one "crazy" patrons who used to aggravate me, but this one was the worst.

Once everything calmed down again, we resumed playing UNO. Somehow the women put their differences aside. Eventually, all seemed to be forgiven, everyone happy once more. I sat there shaking my head in wonder.

Then everything changed again immediately.

Mrs. Hughes and Ms. Randolph marched in, almost at the end of their shifts. To our great shock, they commanded, "Pack all your belongings! You're moving now!"

We gasped in unison, panicking. Where were they taking us? Were they splitting us up? But orders are orders. We were moved as a group, though, to a more spacious tank. The one we departed from held eight inmates. The one we went to was designed for twelve. Peni cried, and I realized they moved us to end her note-passing (later I learned these were "kites") and yelling through the wall, which had been going on constantly as she flirted with a male in the next tank. While I felt sad for her, I was also relieved. The yelling had carried on late into the night, difficult to deal with as continuous as it was. The COs had given Peni many warnings, and they had enough.

Settling into the new tank actually brought a new peace. Friendly games of UNO resumed. A new inmate, Tonya, arrived. We immediately liked her. She was so nice. As the evening unfolded, we discussed faith, related experiences, shared testimony, comforted, and encouraged one another. This part Bahati did not participate in, retreating to her bunk, under her cover.

Tonya explained why she came in, that she was picked up on a two-year-old bond for community service being short by eight hours. She worried about getting back out. We encouraged her in that it probably was a record-keeping issue between the courts and her probation officer because she thought she completed all requirements. She asked each of us about our circumstances. Peni described her abuse issues triggering strong addictions, how her rough life included sexual abuse within her family.

Loreana talked about her previous drug use but how she cleaned up two years prior. Her probation was revoked for getting behind in the fees. This made me contemplate how the probation system is set up for failure, especially for the poor and for those who lose their jobs and go through temporary rough patches. I thought about how I was forced to resign from my job running a public library because of inevitable jail time. I resigned after my lawyer informed me that any kind of alternative sentencing was out of the question. He fought for it by filing continuances for several months, trying to get me a better deal where I could continue my probation or serve time in a work-release program, allowing me to either check into jail for weekends only or serve a combination of evenings and weekends. Before incarceration, I read an article about how more people in Texas choose to serve their sentences in jail because of the stringent requirements of probation.[16] If time served incarcerated would be about half the amount of time spent on probation, and if the poor or unemployed cannot afford the tremendous expense of probation, why not sit the time out in jail? I knew that I, for one, would be relieved after serving my time, when after release, I would be completely done. Once I realized I had to resign from my job anyway, this became exactly what I wanted to do.

"What about you, Shannon?" Tonya drew me back from my musings.

"I'm here for DWI 2 breaking my probation." I briefly recapped the Walmart incident.

"What happened the first time?"

"I got stuck on some railroad tracks down some country road where there was little traffic. I was not spotted for several hours."

"How did you manage that?" she asked in surprise.

"Drinking and driving," I answered. "At some point, I blacked out. I did not know where I was. Finally, a man drove by. I was becoming conscious of my predicament by this time. He turned around, returning to ask me if I needed help. When he approached my vehicle, I rolled down the window, and he could smell the alcohol. 'Been drinking tonight?' he asked. 'Yes,' I affirmed. Then he went away for a bit. I sat there, waiting. I thought he would help me, maybe push my car off the tracks, or call a tow truck and give me a ride. However, soon I saw blue flashing lights in my rearview mirror. As it turns out, he called DPS." (DPS stands for the Department of Public Safety.)

Tonya nodded thoughtfully. "Is this your second time in jail?"

"No, I received a year probated out eighteen months for the original sentence. I was given sixty hours of community service, which I completed, plus I paid off all fines and fees, as well as completing all MHR course requirements." (MHR requirements were completed at the local mental health rehabilitation center.)

"That seems like a stiff sentence for a first-time DWI," commented Tonya.

"That is because my BAC was so high, over 2.0," I explained.

"What's a BAC?" asked Loreana.

"Blood alcohol content."

"Oh," she said.

"So my probation was revoked when I violated it in January by getting a second DWI. The judge sentenced me to a year, including time for both convictions, running concurrently. But you know what?" I asked Tonya.

"What?" she replied.

"My faith is strong. I'm content and happy now. I know God put me here for a purpose. For many reasons. I know most importantly that He used my addiction to get me here. Who would voluntarily quit a good-paying job, end their career, to go to jail?" I asked with a smile, and we all laughed.

"I don't know how you can feel that way," said Tonya. "I'm so anxious and nervous to get out of here."

"Perhaps God needs you here too, just for a very short time, to meet me or Loreana or Peni or all of us. Is that possible?" I asked.

She reflected on this for a moment. "Well, I do have a very strong faith. Perhaps you are right."

"I bet you'll get out tomorrow, no problem. Don't worry. The way I look at it, we can't change our present circumstances. So since I gave my life to God to use me however He wishes, what does He want me to learn from this experience, besides the obvious? What does He want me to do with it?" I remarked.

"You know, I haven't been going to church as much as I used to. I believe in God. Jesus is my Lord and Savior. But I haven't been seeking Him enough lately. Maybe you're right. You've reminded me of my faith. I need to get closer to God again," said Tonya.

"I'm convinced God wanted each of us to meet, probably for more than one reason. When we give ourselves to God totally, submitting our will to His will, giving all control to Him, well, there are no accidents."

"I'm so glad to have met you!" exclaimed Tonya. "I wouldn't have otherwise thought about it like that. I go to a faith-filled church. You should visit it sometime."

"I'd love to!" I agreed. We exchanged church and contact information.

"I want you ladies to give me your information too, to keep in touch. Include your SO numbers so I can compensate you for what you have shared with me," stated Tonya. "Each of you has been so kind, sharing with me your food and other items. If I get out tomorrow, I'm going to contribute to each of your accounts."

"That's so very sweet of you! Thank you!" Tonya knew we each had very little in our accounts. We were all touched. She was released the next day, and later in the afternoon, I noticed my account balance increase by $20.00. *What an angel, what a blessing!* I thought. Since she worked in the nursing field, she had a good income, probably better than the one I had just lost. As we sow, so shall we reap.[17] I spent the past year helping several friends financially when they were in a tight spot, also treating some with low incomes to lunch occasionally.

Peni was listening intently during the entire conversation. She was so moved, she was crying. "I'm a Christian too," she stated. She had the only Bible in the tank, and the others had been borrowing it from her. "I'm so touched by you both. I, too, need to go back to church and get closer to God. I have had so much pain and turmoil for most of my life. I'm tired of hurting."

"Amen!" I exclaimed. "I'm only surviving this because of God. Jesus is the only One who has been able to end the hurts I feel, to soften my heart, fill it with true joy, love, compassion, and to heal me emotionally. Oh, I am far from being fully healed! I know I need treatment, therapy, counseling, or Celebrate Recovery."

"Yes," agreed Tonya, "Twelve-step programs are very helpful. I have been going to CR and AA since 2010, although the local AA meetings can be too negative or depressing. But these programs helped me to get clean. You need to get a sponsor," she said to me.

I nodded, but I was unsure about it. My first sponsor experience did not go so well. I slipped up, and when I told her, she became very angry. Negatively, she told me that my "bottom" would happen when I killed someone in a drunk driving car wreck. She was trying to scare me straight, but she delivered the message with such heated anger that it depressed me. I thought, *If I am ever a sponsor, I'll always speak with love, compassion, and encouragement. Jesus wants us to encourage each other, to lift one another up, not to discourage or tear down.*[18] Thereafter, I stopped attending her AA group, and we never spoke again, although I will always appreciate her effort and the personal time she gave me.

"May I share something with you?" I asked Tonya and Peni specifically; Loreana was no longer participating in the conversation, appearing bored, fiddling with the UNO deck with an impatient expression, wishing we would get back to the game. I did not blame her. UNO is fun, especially playing with these ladies, enjoying their delightful sense of humor.

"Sure!" they answered in unison. I retrieved the book Alex had given me, *The Living Message*, explaining how I had flipped through it earlier as a lark to see what the message was for my sentencing date. "Guess what I found?"

"What?" they asked.

"Jonah and the whale. Jonah was running from God, rebelling, not wanting to do the job God had given him, so God stopped him and confined him. So he had no choice but to be still and listen to God.[19] Coincidence, or is God talking to me?" I asked them.

Looking astonished, Peni said, "Let me see that book! I'm looking up my birth date!" I gave her the book, she read the entry, and said, "You have to read it!" So I did, keeping in mind her background story, saying in response, "I can see how that aptly fits." So Tonya and Loreana looked up their birth dates and agreed and smiled, although they kept any further thoughts to themselves. I felt a flush from head to toe, my skin tingling, and warmth enveloped my body. My eyes teared up.

"Do you feel that?" I asked them. They nodded. Peni wept. Tonya smiled brightly.

"Wow, that's the Holy Spirit!" I said.

"Yes, it is!" they echoed.

"What a night!" I exclaimed happily.

"I was meant to be here also. We all were!" stated Peni. Even Loreana smiled and agreed. After more conversation and a group prayer, we went back to UNO and laughed joyfully into the night, retiring by 2 a.m. As I drifted off to sleep, I felt so warm, happy, content, and excited about the work God had in store for me. I felt Him say, "Look to Me only, lean on Me only. I will supply all of your needs. Do not worry about bills. I will take care of everything." I thanked Him for these lovely ladies, testimonies, and "coincidences" that were actually His communication and for being in a tank where I could be happy, catching up on rest for several weeks before making trustee status. Earlier Loreana and Peni informed me that when I became a trustee, I would be transferred to a trustee-only tank. I wanted to enjoy these ladies more before I had to move.

## MAY 21ST: LETTER TO MY HUSBAND

My dearest Tim,

Day 5

Hey baby! I love you so much! I'm okay! I see why God put me in here. Not just to stop my addiction, give me rest, time to pray, meditate, listen for His instruction, get really close to

Him, but also to have continuous opportunities to witness every day. I know it's going to make for one fantastic book, for which I would seek a Christian publisher. I know in my guts and bones that will be abundantly blessed by God, especially if you lean on Him and trust Him more. No accidents! All a part of His majestic plan.

There have been stressful events, but I came through them fine. A few tears, some frustration, but I survived with God's reassurance and calming presence, along with all the love and compassion He has put in my heart.

I like the tank I'm in. I found out yesterday that if I make trustee, I'll have to move to the trustee tank. This makes me sad because I love my cellmates. The ones I have now are here only for another month, though, so of course, it's all good in the end.

I miss you very much. I miss hugging you and demonstrating my devoted love to you every day. I miss all the dogs, but it probably goes without saying, I especially miss snuggling with Ellis, receiving his kisses.

I am so very grateful for the commissary money. Please, out of my last paycheck, contribute as much as you can to my account. I wish I saved more money for my commissary account. Without it, I scarcely eat. Some trays have nothing on them that I can eat. Most of the time, I take a few bites of a protein that tastes horrible unless it is a hot dog. However, because of your contribution, I was able to get some picante and cheese sauces, which makes what I eat tolerable. I've mentioned my dietary requirements to two nurses. The second one said there's not much they can do about it, i.e., more protein to replace carbs. I didn't expect too much anyway. I can make this work if I can order summer sausage, beef, and cheese sticks. I'm not eating much, but honestly, I'm not too hungry anyway. Thank God for my tiny tummy! I really do hope I lose weight, but I don't think I have so far, which is puzzling. Maybe I'm just bloated. It's also difficult to drink much water. I have to add the flavor packets. I have to remember to drink more as it takes a bit of effort to get the dry, crusty, clumpy powder to dissolve. On the bright side, the packet flavors taste good, and all the ladies have shared with me, so I have enough of them. There's no way that I'm paying commissary prices for beverages. One bottle of water is $1.75! Are you kidding me? When I select items, I try to be as frugal as I can. There are some things that would be nice, but nonessentials are just too much of a luxury on the limited funds. So I am sticking only to essentials.

I already purchased a towel, washcloth, soap, shampoo, boxers, underwear, picante and cheese sauces, beef summer sausage, cheese, one envelope, this notepad, and one stamp.

I ordered vitamins, but they did not arrive, and I was credited for them. If anyone wishes to send me a care package, here is my wish list:

- Creamy peanut butter, Item No. 6417, $5.25
- Summer sausage, Item No. 3585, $3.30
- Velveeta jalapeno cheese spread, Item No. 6444, $3.60
- Tuna pouch, Item No. 6826, $3.45
- Mozzarella cheese bar, Item No. 6459, $2.50
- Cheddar cheese bar, Item No. 6422, $2.50
- Beef Cheese Sticks, Item No. 6320, $1.45
- Twin beef stick, Item No. 6300, $1.45
- BBQ beef, Item No. 6193, $3.65
- Vitamin C, Item No. 0685, $5.00
- Ibuprofen, Item No. 0583, Q. 2 $.75
- Medium size boxers, Item No. 1530, $4.25

- Medium size T-shirt, Item No. 8619, $5.25
- Thermal top medium size, Item No. 1551, $5.25
- Thermal bottoms medium size, Item No. 1561, $5.25
- Cherry cough drops, Item No. 0671, $1.10
- Baby powder, Item No. 0200, $1.25
- Suave moisturizer skin lotion, Item No. 0235
- Washcloth, Item No. 1430, $0.80
- Towel, Item 1441, $1.96
- Hot pot, Item No. 7000, $20.00
- Word search puzzle book, Item No. 4787, $12.00
- Double six dominoes, Item No 1310, $4.00
- Earplugs Q2, Item No 1256, $1.10
- Pen (1"), Item No 1204, $0.95
- Stamped envelopes, Item No. 1001, $0.68
- Letter pad, Item No. 1060, $1.85

I want to focus on the positives! I am housed with "nice" women because when I was processed in, they said I am "nice," haha. We have a hot water shower that stays hot! We have a TV with DIRECTV and FX. We can clean our tank twice a week! We can go outside twice a week for one hour each time! I am joyfully accepting this tough assignment from God! I am safe.

What they give us, to begin with (and what you are "stuck with" if you are indigent), includes:

- a one-inch rubber pen
- one-inch toothbrush (a challenge to use, I assure you!)
- decent size toothpaste tube
- two-inch comb
- tiny bar of soap

- a "Bob Barker" tiny size clear deodorant (hey, look this up: Bob Barker and support for indigent inmates—Google it or something, okay? I find this humorous! All I can think about regarding this is The Price is Right!)
- a tiny towel
- two pairs of tube socks (we only get laundry once a week—phew!)
- two pairs of used panties (I am not kidding!)
- two sports bras (they have seen better days!)
- two T-shirts
- one over-shirt
- one pair orange Crocs
- one roll of toilet paper

We also receive a "Handbook of Rules" (don't lose it, or when you leave, they will charge you $5.00!) and a pamphlet about sexual harassment and zero tolerance... Also, your indigent account is up to $4.00 if I understand correctly. If people put money on your account or send you a care package from the website, you are truly blessed! Oh, and they give you a laundry basket to include all your belongings in. If that ever grows in excess, what the basket can hold, you lose it!

They also issue you a mattress. I am so unlucky! My mattress is so thin! The other ladies have thicker mattresses. I wake up in the morning with sore, aching muscles and bones. That is the only negative I will share with you because I do not want to worry or depress you. Please know that God is giving me the strength to get through this and to come out stronger. But this stupid mattress is like sleeping on concrete. Maybe my judge told the jail to make sure that I am as uncomfortable as possible! Haha!

Following Jesus into Jail

Please mail me a small wallet size picture of you. Thank you so much. I love you so much; I cherish you; you are the best husband in the world!

Your loving wife, Shannon

PS: I am wearing a green bracelet meaning "low-level offender"! I feel like I am at a girl's camp! If anyone wants to send me books, only those from Amazon directly are allowed! I back the blue! I love our first responders! I love our veterans! God bless Texas! God bless the USA!

# CHAPTER 3

# Thursday, May 23rd

## DAY 7: TRUSTEE

Wednesday morning brought another surprising change. After breakfast, I went back to bed and fell into a deep sleep with my newly-arrived earplugs. Bahati shook me awake what felt like a few minutes later, but a couple of hours had passed. Tonya already left for court. I gasped; I was so startled. I went to the door as a CO was calling for me. She turned out to be one who oversees the trustees.

"I'm sorry, ma'am, I was wearing earplugs." I began to explain, but she quickly cut me off with, "Shannon Teichmann?"

"Yes, ma'am?"

"You applied for trustee?"

"Yes, ma'am."

"An opportunity has opened up. Do you still want to be a trustee?"

*This is now or never*, I thought. "Yes, ma'am." I worried if I said I wanted to wait, I wouldn't be offered again, although I would have enjoyed more time with Peni and Loreana.

"Sign this form. You agree that this is of your own free will, and you are not being coerced or forced to work?"

"Okay, yes." I signed the form.

"Okay, pack up; you're going right now."

*Wow*, I thought. Every day brought momentous change. I was disappointed that I would not have more time to rest and relax with the ladies, playing fun card games with them. I envisioned the work as being hard labor and prayed I was up to it. They say that opportunity never knocks twice (not that I truly believe that), so it was now or never, and I wanted two-for-one badly. The thought of getting out and back home to my husband and fur babies by November instead of the following April was highly appealing.

So I packed fast and sadly said quick goodbyes with hugs and promises to keep in touch. I asked Peni to tell Tonya goodbye for me. I don't know where I thought I was going. The trustee tank was just across the hallway. I laughed when I realized this. *Surely I'll see the ladies again soon in rec or serving trays then.* I pictured moving to the other side of the jail or maybe an annex or outside building. I imagined even getting an office job because of my highly technical skillset and literacy level. Oh, how "newbie" I was! So naive! Hey, I was new to incarceration. In the fifty years leading up to this, I never got in any trouble beyond that of a speeding ticket. I soon found out that there are only two jobs offered to females: cleaning and serving food trays.

I felt intimidated going into the trustee tank. Peni had exclaimed, "But they're so mean!" when she realized I was leaving to be one. Renee, a young, pretty woman with red, curly hair, green eyes, and rosy, plump cheeks, escorted me into the trustee tank. She introduced me to the other women after waking them. Kristy from the holding tank was also becoming a trustee. When Renee informed the women that they needed to make room for two new bunks by clearing their stuff off the top ones, my first impression was that these ladies were unfriendly. They seemed grumpy and unwelcoming, groaning as they roused. *Trustees work hard and require more sleep*, I surmised. I realized why they were sleepy: that some of them worked late into the night or multiple shifts. They sleep when they can. I was just deeply asleep myself. I find it quite hard to wake up from a nice, sweet slumber.

Only two top bunks were available. Kristy chose the one against the wall, and I chose the other on the first set. As it turned out, Renee had the bunk below that one, so I was happy with the arrangement because she seemed so nice. She took responsibility for training me, and we went on my first shift that night cleaning. One of the nicer, more relaxed COs was on duty, so it was a straightforward introduction to the cleaning responsibilities. Ah yes, I know, cleaning is not rocket science. However, performing these duties under the watchful eyes of the guards could be stressful, especially those who correct sharply for slow or incorrectly completed tasks.

I quickly bonded with Renee. We have an easy rapport. She is witty and funny. We spontaneously laugh together. She is patient as I grill her on my responsibilities, asking all kinds of questions on how best to perform duties. We talk about our faith and life experiences. As we conversed at one of the tank's tables after work, she looked lovely in the dim lighting, having an earnest, open expression. She endured far worse in life than I, abused in the home beginning from a young age, with adults taking advantage of her vulnerability, spurning drug use from her preteen years. She has a background similar to Peni's.

I relate to these young women on some level, although I never used illegal substances. My drinking at home was legal, as my sentencing judge pointed out. My crime was operating a moving vehicle on public roads while inebriated, potentially putting other lives at risk. Most of the women I met in jail abused illegal substances, as well as manufactured and/or distributed them. I relate to my tankmates at the level of experiencing life traumas. I survived five rape attempts during my teenage years, from age twelve to nineteen. An accumulation of life traumas without treatment and counseling seems to be the theme in these conversations.

The easy rapport I experience with Renee leads to intimate confessions of past sinful behavior. She enjoys a close relationship with another tankmate who identifies as a male and prefers to be referred to as such. Raven convinces me of his assumed gender in looks, mannerisms, and deep voice. He looks to be no more than eighteen. My impression of their relationship is that of a mother and son. Renee is in her mid-twenties. The affection I observe between them seems neutral in light touching, caressing each other's arms. I caressed my son's arm when he was young, so for me, that was motherly affection. Before retiring this evening, the three of us laughed, joked, and talked about life. I am smiling with warm fuzzies. I thank God for a good day.

# CHAPTER 4
# Thursday, May 23rd

## LETTER TO MY HUSBAND

My dear, sweet husband,

Day 7

Today, as you know, is our fifth anniversary. I am with you in spirit. I will call you soon.

I received donations, so I ordered food, such as beef sticks, cheese, and summer sausage, which should tide me over between meals. Four requests for a protein substitute to soy have been denied. I did not realize I was eating soy for a few days but wondered why my stomach hurt and my belly swelled to twice its size. I laid down for a long time to get as comfortable as possible until the discomfort passed. Hey, at least I will lose my twenty extra pounds and look great! Ha!

Do not worry. I'm happy and excited. God's plan for me is coming to fruition. The future looks brighter. Moving to the trustee tank is a blessing. I'm bonding with everyone in here, and I'm delighted they are quiet and keep the noise level to a minimum. What a relief! I'm in training for cleaning and serving trays. It's hard, but I'm sure I will catch on and get the hang of it. I'm too slow! I've got to speed up!

I am going to take an eight-week Bible study, and I have two Bible studies now and a daily devotional. I'm going to take a Life Recovery class in June, where I will be given a Life Recovery Bible (which I will only receive upon completion). I will go to everything I can. Everyone I am with now is in recovery. I think this is the best thing that could've happened to me. I'm grateful the nightmare is over. I just could not escape the death trap of alcoholism. With AA and CR on top of work with all of its pressures, including pressures at home—you know what I mean. I can no longer allow myself to be subject to abuse from anyone. Thank God you escaped that problem and are loving, kind, and compassionate. At any rate, henceforth, I must be honest and stop biting my tongue, swallowing everything. I must stand up for myself.

I have a big favor to ask of you. I need the ability to worship God in song while I am in here. Please do this for me. Print the lyrics to these songs and mail them to me so I can sing them with my tankmates. We are all Christians and would love to be able to sing praises to God. I love you immensely and appreciate you greatly!

- "Lights Shine Bright" by TobyMac
- "Love Broke Thru" by TobyMac
- "Come to the Table" by Sidewalk Prophets
- "Reckless Love of God" by Rick Asbury
- "So Will I (1,000 Billion X)" by Hillsong
- "Bulletproof" by Citizen Way
- "Breakup Song" by Francesca Battistelli
- "Good Good Father" by Big Daddy Weave
- "Redemption" by MercyMe
- "Redeemed" by Big Daddy Weave

PS: If anyone tells you they donated to my account, please tell them that I am so very grateful! Know that I'm happy, positive, cheerful, witnessing, writing prolifically, learning so much! I miss you incredibly, along with our fur babies! I love you forever and always!

# CHAPTER 5

# Friday, May 24th

## DAY 8: ROLLED

After waking this morning at 6 a.m. for medicines and breakfast, I returned to sleep. Putting my earplugs in, I drifted off deeply. I tossed and turned during the night because Renee shared her coffee with me last evening, which was the first caffeine I drank in a while. When I consume caffeine in the evening, sleep evades me. I should have known better than to chance a good night's rest, but the coffee concoction made with added cappuccino, hot chocolate, an atomic fireball, and butter-scotch candy is delicious. So this morning, I slept hard for several hours. When I came to, I was informed that I "missed every-thing." The other girls pointed out the empty spaces to my left where Renee had slept on the floor and Raven in the next bunk.

"They were rolled this morning," Tammy informed me. "You slept through all of it. We were surprised you didn't wake up." I was surprised too. I was groggy, trying to absorb this new development as my head cleared.

"Why?" I finally managed to ask.

"Because I caught them in inappropriate behavior, right there on the floor next to you, where I could see them, and you could have also if you had woken up. You were facing them but slept through it, thank God. I'm like, 'No, you ain't gonna disrespect her like that,' and I reported it," Tammy explained.

"So, 'rolled' means returned to the general population?" I asked.

"Yes."

"Ah." I was shocked and felt very naive again. I had no idea. I knew Raven was gay but misunderstood their relationship. They are "more than friends." I am not a judgmental person. As Jesus said, "Do not judge, or you will be judged."[20] He also instructs us to love everyone.[21] I am disappointed that they took this chance and were kicked out as I enjoyed their company. The past two days revealed strife between Renee and Tammy, but I was not cognizant of the extent of animosity between them. I would say that Tammy is in the right because she has been here longer and is older. Renee should have respected her and deferred to her seniority, but she called Tammy "bossy." Tammy can be gruff and has a commanding tone while training others, but as fast as one has to be in order to meet the COs' expectations, it is understandable. However, I miss them. I pray for their growth, healing, maturity, and future adherence to rules. As intelligent as they are, breaking the rules in jail is not smart.

So yes, once again, life in jail is full of daily surprises.

# CHAPTER 6

# May 30th

## LETTER TO MY HUSBAND

My dearest husband,

Day 14

In all of the world, I love you so much! I will keep this short. You are welcome!

Please mail me the following (I hope this list helps, not trying to rush or pressure you):

- family photo (not larger than 9x10);
- song lyrics of praise worship music;
- reduction of surcharges form completed by you, ready for me to sign;
- unsworn declaration by inmate by same site; I need by DL number;
- the medical POAs and Last Will and Testament already prepared, ready for witnesses and notary;
- my vitamin Rx info;
- contact information—I need addresses and numbers to send thank you notes.

I am terribly sorry, darling, to put all of this on you. I should have taken care of it ahead of time, but I was under so much pressure with a short deadline, I failed to think of this regarding vitamins and surgery information. Please forgive me! XOXO.

Your loving wife, Shannon, a.k.a. Me2

## LETTER TO MY SISTER

Dear Lisa,

Day 14

I'm deeply grateful for all your help and support. I'm blown away by all the love, help, and support that I'm receiving! Thank you so much for the care package!

It was a pleasure speaking with you on the phone. If only it weren't so expensive! But I didn't know we could make calls from our tank! What a wonderful privilege.

Time is moving fast. I've been in two weeks tomorrow. In the meantime, I'm resting, meditating, and praying. I'm listening to that small, still, quiet voice. I was given a Bible and other material, including a workbook for prisoners about finding God's purpose for our lives. It fits in perfectly with what I was already thinking—why God put me here.

In retrospect, as I look back, I was so exhausted. I was cracking. I went directly from one job just after major surgery with one week off only, when six weeks recuperation was recommended. Then I took a two-thousand-mile road trip to see my son graduate boot camp, spent only two nights on the road, went directly to a new job where my first task was to move the entire library after downsizing the collection by ninety percent, packing four hundred plus boxes for storage for an auction that never took place and moved what I decided to keep to a new location. Then I set up the new library in the space of only a few months. Thereafter, I never stopped running constantly, working hard, servicing an average of one hundred Pro Se patrons per week, processing one hundred inmate requests weekly, and cataloging and maintaining four thousand Pro Se forms.

After the crazy horse lady was banned from the courthouse for harassing all departments contained therein (with me the most of all, driving me insane!), the rest of the patrons came flooding back, and boom! Busy, busy, busy! I loved it! Time flew by! God empowered me to do an excellent job. I was able to encourage, comfort, and lift spirits every day. I was often told, "You're an angel!" or "You're the kindest person I've ever met!" Very gratifying and humbling!

I was running on fumes. As a newbie, I had very few days off, either in vacation or sick time, only a few holidays all year. I commuted ten hours a week. I felt so much pressure on me trying to keep everyone at work, home, and next door happy, always feeling like the target of someone's resentment. I just cracked. Mid-life crisis? Emotional/mental breakdown? Not sleeping well. Later, long weekends at Goodwill completing community service.

By the weekend of January 27th, I crashed and burned. I was drinking. I skipped church with the intention of snuggling with Ellis on the couch all day. When Tim insisted I go to the store, I begged him not to make me, "That's why I'm not in church this morning. I'm exhausted. Please don't make me go."

His response was, "I don't have time! I have too much else to do, and I need cracked black pepper for dinner. You're not doing anything else! Just go to the nearby Dollar General." I couldn't believe he couldn't tell I was drinking. He previously told me he could always tell even if I had only one sip of wine. I was too embarrassed and ashamed to tell him the truth. It's not his fault I decided to go to Greenville so I could buy wine. I wasn't in my right mind. The rest is history.

My mother-in-law sent me a card saying she loves me, she's behind me, and she'll make sure that I don't go hungry in here. She has a soft heart now. Tim's sister called him yesterday. She doesn't ask about me, but that is okay. Pray for me, though. Pray for me that I can let go of resentment for anyone who I think hurt me. I must completely forgive everyone in my life I ever felt hurt by, past, present, and future. I appreciate your prayers.

I have been writing a lot and these short, rubber safety pens cramp my hand, so I will close now. I am happy and excited for my future and the great blessings that will follow when I do the work God has for me.

XOXO.

Love always, Shannon

# CHAPTER 7

# June 3rd

## LETTER TO MY SISTER

Dear Lisa,

Day 18

Hey Sis! Tim called Dad because he called my mother-in-law looking for me. He panicked when I didn't return his calls. Tim filled him in on where I'm at and why. Dad was very mad, not at me but at the justice system. He wishes I called him and told him because he would have hired me a lawyer, "the best there is." I did not tell Dad because I didn't want to break his heart. I should have rather than making assumptions. He offered to help us financially. The years have softened his heart.

Could you do me a favor? The one thing I ran out of time to take care of the loan against my retirement, TIAA-CREF. Can you see if there is a way to pause payments temporarily? I drained my retirement trying to stay out of jail, and here I sit anyway! What a colossal waste of money! I know God has great things in store for me and that all will be well. God wakes me up in the middle of the night when it's quiet, and, wide awake, I write for an hour or two and then return to bed. I have written sixty pages so far, probably about thirty typed pages. It just flows!

I can't make any more calls right now until Tim puts more money on my books. I want to be careful, to stretch it out for food essentials. Thank you so much for the care package! I was so blown away by all the kindness and generosity, and yours on top of all that you are already doing for me!

I know that prosperity is coming by doing what God wants me to, and I'll be able to pay back everything with interest. I know you told me not to worry about it. I feel so much peace, comfort, and joy. I feel excited for what the future brings. I always wanted to be a writer and artist. I never had a "story" until now. I think He's putting great ideas in my mind now.

I have "blue" moments, but I meditate to chase them away. Sometimes I feel I am in a girl's summer camp when I'm sitting on my bunk talking about life, music, movies, etc., with my tankmates. Other times I feel like I'm in boot camp when I am obeying strict (but fair) guards in subservient required ways (face wall, hands behind back, head down, etc.). Sometimes it feels like high school, passing out food trays (of purely tasteless garbage, you know, all bread and "schmeat," a.k.a. soy meat that my dogs would turn down and anemic vegetables swimming around in pools of water). I'm so blessed and grateful for the meat gifts! I signed up to see a doctor for $20, who could prescribe a special tray with real protein, and I have plenty now to eat meanwhile.

Receiving the coffee was thrilling. What a big difference that makes when I get up at 5 a.m. for meds and the morning work shift. Luckily a tankmate has a hot pot, especially since they cost $20; they are essential to heat water for the coffee and food pouches from the commissary. I might lose all three tankmates any time now as one goes to the state for a year (bless her!), and one may get out on bail. That makes me nervous because I could be required to work all three shifts training everyone new, but then I could take the best bunk by the wall and have seniority. Hopefully, that helps if a new girl comes in who is a bully, domineering, or controlling. However, I'm thinking positive. Every woman I've met so far loves me because I'm so loving and friendly. I don't anticipate trouble. I love you! Thanks again for everything!

Shannypoo

# CHAPTER 8

# Tuesday, June 4th

## DAY 19

Over the past week and a half, opportunities for sharing ministry, witnessing, testimony, encouragement, comforting and loving, continued. Kristy, my holding tankmate, wants out badly. She begs her mother, father, friends, anyone she contacts on the outside to post her bail. Most of them are stringing her along, promising every day to get her out, always failing to do so, causing her emotional turmoil. I pray for her constantly, for any of them to make good on their promises or to just be honest with her that they are not going to help her. Tammy and Ruth share my skepticism that she will be released. We hope for our sake she will because her anguish and our failed attempts to calm her down keep the atmosphere tense and uncomfortable.

Soon after being incarcerated, I was given a book by Katie Souza,[22] who explains that every judge and earthly authority is appointed by God.[23] He controls everything and uses our modern legal system to "exile" us in jails and prisons for His purposes,[24] including the opportunity for us to turn away from our sin, seek a close relationship with Him, and work in the future to advance His kingdom here on earth. This workbook is extremely applicable and helpful, falling right in line with what God is whispering to me. He put me here to restore my health, give me rest, break my craving for alcohol, with enough time to completely eliminate it from my system, detoxifying my body. He is restoring my soul, mending my relationship with Him, preparing me for His purposes: to enter ministry, to advance His causes, kingdom, help lead others to His light while I learn from them.

Impressed with this work, I recommended it to Kristy, who is beginning to realize no one is going to post bail for her. For her sake, I am glad because I think if they do, most likely, she will return directly back to her drug-infused lifestyle, manufacturing, selling, and using. From night one in the cold, dirty holding tank, watching her sleep on the floor, God moved me with compassion. I did not understand what He might be saying at the time, not knowing that we would have more time together soon with both of us becoming trustees, but I felt Him insist that when the opportunity presented itself, speak to her about Him.

I did at the first chance, thinking then it would be the *only* chance. We were waiting in the hallway for processing into the general population, where she was crying, very upset, saying she wanted to go into a treatment program. When I caught her eye, I said that I knew of a free Christian women's home in Fort Worth, but it required a minimum of six months' commitment. I asked her if the "Christian thing" would bother her, at which point she said, "No, at this point, I'll try anything."

Then I said, "I will keep you in my prayers. Trust it will get better, that there is light at the end of the tunnel."

"Thank you," she replied. After that, we were classified (i.e., low, medium, or high risk with appropriately colored wristbands, green, orange, or red, respectively) and sent into different tanks. After we met again as trustees the following Wednesday morning, we had more opportunities to talk. We both are reading and discussing Souza's book, comparing faith experiences and past painful events. I hope God is working through me to reclaim one of His precious children. Our talks are mutually beneficial. She was raised going to church and knew the Bible quite well, better than I do. I learn so much from her story and testimony.

Ruth and I also share faith, testimony, similar experiences, tragedies, unfortunate events, and God's saving grace in our lives. She is working through Souza's book too. I read *The Insanity of God* by Nik Ripkin[25] and passed it on to Ruth as my avid attention to the book intrigued her. Ripkin's work is humbling, describing the persecution Christians worldwide suffer and endure, making me think about the anemic state of American churches. I summarized the content for Ruth, and she said that her son ministers overseas also, doing similar work, gathering testimony from persecuted Christians, so she is keen to read it. I would put it on a must-read list for anyone who sincerely follows Christ, desiring to devote their lives to His service. Ruth is a smart woman. She has been far more successful in life than I ever was. She used to be an engineer for L3. Between her and her husband, they grossed $300,000 a year at one point. What a shame they began to experience marital stress and became involved in the drug community, eventually leading to where she is at now. I am not the only one here who achieved a higher level in life than many others with whom we are incarcerated.

I go to rec when I have the next opportunity to be with others from the general population. When I saw Renee, I was both happy and on edge, knowing she would grill me about her expulsion from the trustee tank. She ran up to me and hugged me.

"I miss you!" she exclaimed.

"I miss you, too."

"So what did they tell you?" *Oh boy*, I thought. *I don't want to have this conversation.* After initially telling me that she reported them, Tammy later denied it and told me to tell Renee she had nothing to do with it should I run into her. Tammy does not want to be held responsible. This put me in the uncomfortable position of either trying to avoid the truth without lying or to go against Tammy's wishes and just tell Renee the truth. Tammy should stand behind what she did. I decided that ultimately, honesty is the best policy.

"That you and Raven had relations on the floor between bunks."

"That's a lie!" I looked at her dubiously. "Who told you that?"

"They both did," I answered cautiously, which was true enough, referring both to Tammy and Ruth.

"But it was Tammy who reported it, wasn't it? She woke up. I know she did." I thought, *Well, you're contradicting yourself, now, aren't you?* Renee continued, "But she didn't see anything! I was under cover." *So, in reality, you are confessing,* I thought.

"I am not entirely sure who reported it," I responded.

"Had to be Tammy. She had it in for me."

"Probably was her," I answered, wishing I weren't caught in this drama but thinking that Renee knew the truth of the matter anyway. *I should have just said yes from the start,* I thought.

"How is Raven doing?"

"I don't know."

"Haven't you seen Raven?"

"I saw him only briefly when serving trays the other day."

"Did he look sad?" I nodded, and with that, she was off to talk to someone else.

The next time I saw Renee at rec, she was not doing well with their separation. She had to spend two nights in solitary after arguing with another inmate. My heart goes out to her. I keep praying for her to overcome her challenges and to stop breaking rules, causing dire consequences. I was the only trustee to go to rec. I wondered why the others would not join me until I saw Renee in the yard, and then I was grateful they did not join me. I am uncomfortable with others fighting with each other or with me. What I thought was a light flirtation between Renee and Raven has become evident to me it is more serious. Renee discussed her feelings, expressing just how much she misses him. When I heard the other trustees say that Raven has other girlfriends in every tank and one "at home" also, I was skeptical Raven feels the same way about Renee. However, as Renee and I walked in a circle, we came across a message on the ground made with paint chips from the peeling walls, clearly reading, "Raven loves Renee." She stared at it for a moment in stunned silence and declared, "See, he loves me too!" I feel compassion for them both. I still wish they complied with the rules so they could be together and I could still be enjoying their company in the trustee tank.

Renee asked me to pass a note (or "kite") to Raven, but I politely declined. I explained that I would not take the chance to be caught and rolled. No one else is as important to me as my husband, aside from God and my son. Going home by November is essential. She said she understood and did not show any resentment.

---

Another time at rec, I struck up a conversation with an older woman named Francis. She has long gray hair and pretty blue eyes. She discussed her view of local authorities targeting people with prior convictions and how her relatives who were convicted of drug charges faced subsequent arrests where police planted evidence. She claimed that law enforcement continually harasses people "in the system." She told me she is guilty of the DWIs for which she is convicted, but she was referring to her son and other relatives. Recently, Ruth related similar thoughts about her own interactions with law enforcement. "It happens all the time!" Francis declared. She explained she is headed to SAF-P, facing six months there followed by two years at state. My heart goes out to her. She is at peace with it, however, as I am with my sentence. "After all," she added thoughtfully, "I could have hurt or killed someone, and I thank God daily for protecting others and myself from that from happening."

"Me too!" I exclaimed.

"Only God is getting me through this."

"Me too!" I repeated. "I'm glad to be here and have the madness over," I confessed. "I was exhausted. I loved my job and hated to leave it, but between all the stress and not having any downtime, I reached my breaking point. I think that is largely why I was drinking so much. I was having an emotional break-down. I had very few days off work and a long commute. But," I stressed, "work was also a haven for me. Other stressors took their toll," I told her.

"Are you married?" Francis asked.

"Yes, but I have a great marriage. He's wonderful and very patient with me. He loves me so much; he stands by me through thick and thin, even when he is told that he shouldn't." She nodded at that, questioning no further. "But I still feel so much pain for all the mistakes I made. I was so selfish. I was bitter, too, toward those who 'did me wrong.' I was resentful and angry. I carried around so much baggage. Then, a few years ago, I was saved, and that changed everything. I healed emotionally. I was freed from anger and resentments that were binding me. Jesus filled my heart with so much love, compassion, and forgiveness. I flew high as a kite as a baby Christian the first year. But then things happened after that, which killed the high. I began drinking again because of emotional pain. I was regretting past mistakes where I could have done things so much better if only I stayed close to God my whole life. When I felt that pain, I just wanted to numb it."

"I totally get that," Francis replied. Suddenly she asked, "Will you pray for me since I'm going to state?"

"Sure," I answered. "I still am not eloquent in prayer, but I'm happy to." She put out her hands, and I took them, and I hoped to find the right words to say, asking God for help. "Dear most heavenly Father Abba, most holy God on high, I lift Francis up to You, speaking peace, protection, and blessings over her, as she heads to the next leg in her journey. Please comfort her, keep her warm and safe in Your embrace, with angels surrounding her. We are so grateful for Your kind, tender mercies, Father. We praise You and thank You for everything. In Jesus' sweet, precious name, I pray, amen."

"Amen," said Francis. "Thank you, Shannon."

"You're very welcome."

At that, the CO called us back in as rec time ended.

---

Ruth has taught me the cleaning and food service routines. We take morning shifts and Kristy and Tammy evenings. The work is humbling. I feel in my gut Jesus saying, "I need you to be empathetic with the most humble, those who have it the hardest." I say "feel" because my communications from God are usually "gut feelings" at my core. I know this innately, without doubt. Whenever in my life I didn't obey my "gut instinct," things went wrong, often terribly. From there, the interpretation into words comes naturally. Cleaning and serving meals humbles me because of the stern guards. I feel intimidated and fear I will screw up, get yelled at, and then cry, mortified. Crying in public is one of the most humiliating experiences. I never cry at appropriate times, such as at funerals, when my eyes stay as dry as Texas in August. No, I cry at work. In the past, if a boss or coworker yelled at me, I cried, felt ashamed of it, and hid in the bathroom.

Ruth says inmates must display subservient respect at all times. Heads down, don't make eye contact, face the wall when told to, when higher rank is on the floor, and when officials or male inmates approach. Hold your hands behind your back. No looking at, flirting with, or smiling at male inmates whatsoever. Renee was yelled at for this more than once when I worked with her.

Completing routine steps in the correct order challenges me. I forget little things like propping the door open for the other worker. The kitchen carts are big, heavy, and best navigated with two people. When I had to push one down the hallway by myself, it was awkward until I got the knack of pushing it sideways. Strength is required to navigate it around corners, and it easily careens off course and bangs into the wall. I imagine the horror I would feel if I lost control and knocked over the CO.

As I catch on, the work becomes easier. The hardest part is avoiding being yelled at for being slow or making mistakes. I am learning each CO's manner, which ones are stricter, more laid back, and their preferences. Each CO differs in the order tasks should be completed, such as whether to clean first, then serve, then clean again, or "fake" clean for the cameras but truly speed through it. The COs' approach to rule enforcement is inconsistent among them. They keep me on my toes.

---

Commissary day following Memorial Day was exciting since we had to wait longer than usual for our orders, the warehouse being closed for the holiday. Kristy was unhappy that day as she was unable to order anything and knew nothing unexpected would arrive for her. I can understand feeling left out. I felt that way much of my life, struggling financially among a prosperous family. However, I was showered with gifts this day with four care packages from my family and husband. The commissary lady said this was a record. I am overwhelmed, blown away, deeply touched, and humbled. Mrs. Hughes was grumpy because it took extra trips helping bring the stuff to the female floor. The gifts included proteins, such as summer sausage, to supplement my diet. I received luxuries such as lotion and chocolate. I shared with Kristy some items I previously acquired, hoping to soften her difficult day. I grasped just how truly blessed I had a loving, supporting family on the outside, something Kristy was truly missing. Even if she never entered the drug world, her family sounded truly awful, uncaring, some of the worst parents a person could have. Her mother was still a crack addict, apparently.

Oh, the things I took for granted before my trip to jail! I hope that those who never break the law, drink and drive or live in the drug world count their blessings. These inmates experienced the fear and pain of total isolation, resulting from abandonment, tragic loss through losing parents via death, or being raised by hateful losers who reject their kids, who, in turn, become a part of street life. They were sucked into a life of prostitution and drugs just to survive and cope, to find shelter, for which they paid with their bodies. Such has life been for Kristy and many of the others I have met. They suffered extreme abuse from young ages. Kristy's abuser got her pregnant at age twelve. She had her first child at thirteen. She has been in and out of the system since then. For those whose hearts are unmoved by compassion with stories like hers, their hearts are, indeed, hard and far from God.

In my mind, I can hear a dozen voices among family, friends, and the guards, saying, "Well, they deserve to be in jail, and it's not supposed to be comfortable or fun!" True, but what would Jesus say? Love and compassion would certainly move Him. He came for the lowly, the least of thieves, sinners, beggars, poorest, tax collectors, and even murderers.[26] [27] This is how I feel. Jesus put so much compassion in my heart, my "cup runneth over,"[28] and I must share it with everyone I meet. I believe this is the true way to win lost souls over to God, to pull them out of darkness into the light, by showing mercy, compassion, caring, His great love without judgment. Remember Jesus's instruction, "Let him who is without sin among you be the first to cast a stone at her."[29] Who among us is perfect like Jesus? The one who says, "I am," is blind, but even this is forgivable if said person knows not what he does.[30] God forgives those who seek Him. Although we should forgive regardless, as it is not our place to judge, God would forgive said person if she or he would open his or her heart and *ask* for forgiveness.[31] This is why Jesus came for the lost: because their hearts are capable of opening to Him to experience His love, healing, comfort, and light. As for the Pharisees and scribes, "… their hearts are far from me."[32] We have plenty of them in our modern day. The haughty, arrogant, have-it-all, those who never had a bad moment in life, unknowing, unseeing, whose hearts are hard as stone. Those who do not believe in Him at all, or those who claim to "hate" Him, "hate" Jesus, and resent Christians.

However, Jesus teaches us to love everyone[33], even those just described and those who hurt us and would be enemies.[34] Even those who are arrogant, hateful, or are lost souls, pray for them and love them with the love of Christ.[35] This is the answer I give to those who say, "Well, they deserve it and more! They broke the law! They should be in pure misery!" To be honest with you, having experienced it, just being caged like an animal twenty-four seven with few, if any, trips to a small concrete yard to breathe fresh air and stare at a small patch of sky for one hour, once or twice a week, is miserable. Knowing there is no escape, and even if one managed it, she or he would be back soon enough and incarcerated for even a greater length of time. Even for those who run from the law, they are not truly free, always on the run, fearful of being caught, having to assume a false identity, and constantly looking over their shoulders; where is the "freedom" in that? I am not saying that inmates are undeserving of confinement, sanctions, and punishment. Just as Souza talked about, God uses the legal system to stop them.

This subject reminds me of some of Bernard B. Kerik's discussions in *From Jailer to Jailed.* At one point, he writes about his time at Cumberland: "The inmate next to me complained about the mice and rats, and a guard basically told him, 'Get over it, you're in jail; this is how it's supposed to be.' I heard this and thought, No, that's not the answer; the answer is that we're not supposed to be living in nat waste."[36] As Kerik succinctly puts it later in the book:

> ... subjected to humiliating strip searches, poor
> sanitary conditions, an unhealthy diet and arbi-

trary and capricious administrating of antiquated and draconian rules... people... say that inmates shouldn't have televisions, sports activities, or any other amenity. They have no idea how moronic that is. If you take away all these small, basic things so that there is absolutely nothing for inmates to do, you just expedite the institutionalization of these men and women, diminish their social values even more, and really turn them into monsters before you return them to society.[37]

I agree with him in that losing freedom and being confined *is* the punishment. Additional punitive measures designed to make inmate life miserable serve no constructive purpose. Kerik is not writing from a Christian viewpoint, however. The one difference between his thoughts on incarceration and mine is that, as Souza talks about in her book, confinement serves a positive purpose when inmates take the opportunity to study God's Word and come to Christ, discovering their divine purpose for which God created them.

---

Today was melancholy. Ruth has not left yet, or "pulled" to SAF-P, a state prison for addiction designed as an alternative to regular incarceration in the Texas Department of Criminal Justice (TDCJ). She is anxious about moving on to the next leg of her "adventure." Tammy is depressed because she anticipated getting out on a personal recognizance (PR) bond, only to find out she is indicted and will be held. She hoped for probation, but it was not offered at this morning's hearing. A new hearing is scheduled for June 27th. She just wants to go home to her husband, not understanding all the charges brought against her (she claims) and her possible resulting sentence. She says that her court-appointed lawyer is rude, uncaring, and is unwilling to elucidate what exactly is happening. Furthermore, her husband was not at the hearing; apparently, he never attends them and is unwilling to bail her out or hire another lawyer.

I am truly blessed to have a husband who stands by me, who bailed me out twice, always attended my hearings, held my hand, and wept when my judge handed out a stiff sentence of a year. No doubt Tammy's husband loves her, but he just told her to "do her time." Kristy continues to be frustrated that no one in her family or circle of friends is bailing her out. I have three despondent tankmates who wish they were anywhere else and probably will be with me a while. I just never know day to day what will change or what anticipated changes will fail to take place. We expect the addition of a new trustee soon, one who has applied. Kristy and Ruth both know her. Kristy thinks she is a good choice. Ruth is unsure, fearing the younger woman will bring drama. I just hope she will be quiet, or at least not *too* loud, and will also be respectful.

Ruth described the harassment and false charges brought against her forty-eight times in this county, matching Francis's story about her son's harassment. Both women told me how common it is, expressing their opinion of the corruption level. I realize inmate claims of corruption and rearrests with planted evidence must be viewed with skepticism lacking solid evidence that this takes place, but it would not surprise me if this type of thing happens not just here but throughout the country. On the other hand, I believe a majority of law enforcement consists of good officers with only a few who become corrupt, as with any group in society. I want to make it clear that I "back the blue," appreciate, and support the police and other first responders. That said, even a CO told me that now I am convicted, I am "in the system" and have put a target on my back. She warned me to be very careful because if I am pulled over in the future, there could be much more suspicion of me.

Peni looks despondent during the brief times I glimpse her. She was moved to a different tank from Loreana's after they argued and apparently were separated due to their fighting. As trustee, at times, I go into the tanks to gather trays and garbage. Peni does not even look up. I want to talk to her, but two of the COs, Mrs. Hughes and Ms. Connor, forbid the trustees to speak with other inmates during work. Other COs are relaxed about that. I hope to see Peni at rec, but she never goes. I remember her hug and how she told me that I comforted her. My heart aches for all these women, and I continue to lift them up in prayer, begging God to bring them peace and comfort as well as acceptance of their situations. Ruth is looking at either six or nine months at SAF-P, while Peni is facing several years. Tammy may be incarcerated another year. I do not know what Kristy's sentence will be. She says someone told her she could be doing up to twenty-five years. This shocks me. These are all drug use and manufacturing charges with intent to distribute. I wonder if I am right thinking that rapists and perpetrators of assault, armed robbery, and other serious, violent crimes receive less time. Given my experience here, I have a new interest in criminal justice reform, which I think is greatly needed in our society.

Actually, I became interested in criminal justice reform at my last job as a law librarian. I am melancholic because I miss that position where I was so capable, establishing a small public library by downsizing it considerably to fit into a limited physical space, but thus modernizing it by transferring most of the collection from paper to digital form. I amazed myself at the good job I did, but I know it was all God, and I give Him all the credit and glory. I was a librarian for fifteen-plus years, but I lacked this subject-specific background. Ten years ago, I could not have accomplished this task when I was not walking with God, seeking a close, intimate relationship with Him. My spiritual journey back to God began in 2013 when the History Channel aired *The Bible*. God anointed and blessed this program, produced by Roma Downey and Mark Burnett;[38] it was so moving, beautiful, touching me deeply, planting seeds of thirst for Jesus in my soul.

I miss greeting patrons with warmth and a big smile as they entered the library, asking them, "What can I help you with today?" I had ample opportunities to testify, witness, share God's love, shine His light to people hurting from marital splits, divorce proceedings, custody battles, death in the family, and those in need of probate forms or who had other dramatic circumstances. Most of my patrons could be comforted, encouraged, uplifted, and walked out feeling more hopeful than when they arrived. Only a very small minority remained untouched, enraged, dissatisfied. Some insulted me, saying, "You obviously don't know what you are doing!" Usually said in response to my explanation that I was not a lawyer and could not provide legal advice, that I would actually break Texas law by doing so. A librarian, staff, even paralegals cannot provide legal advice in Texas if not a practicing lawyer with active membership in the State Bar of Texas.

I explained daily, tediously, my role as a librarian to guide patrons to where they could search for and locate forms, statutes, case law, and other secondary sources located in databases and other resources. When I explained this, most people understood and appreciated my reassurance that I *did* want to help them within legal parameters. The satisfaction my patrons expressed was deeply gratifying. I thanked God daily, hourly even. I opened my day with prayer, "God, please work through me today. Speak through me, help me to remember one of a million details that will help each of my patrons today. I claim this space in the name of Jesus Christ. His light fills this room, and nothing negative can stay or enter in here. In Jesus' name, I always pray, amen." I anointed myself and the room with blessed oil of Frankincense and Myrrh, lovely aromas. Many times patrons commented on how light and good the "vibes" felt in the room.

I was in love with the job, which became my haven (at least when the horse-lady was absent). I pictured myself working there until retirement. I loved my wardrobe too. I enjoyed dressing up pretty for the public, with cute shoes, matching jewelry, and coordinated accessories. I usually wore crosses, fish, and other Christian symbols for earrings, rings, and necklaces, to quietly say, "I am a person of faith." Perhaps I began to love the job itself, its status, and my beautiful wardrobe too much. I was forced to resign from it, sadly, way too soon when I saw the writing on the wall…six months to a year of jail time for my addiction and subsequent lawbreaking. I fought hard and argued vehemently for work release, weekends, extended probation, additional fees and fines, a million hours of community service, anything, to allow me to keep working, as I was so passionate about this job and good at it by the glory and grace and God.

However, I turned my life over to God a few years before. The joy I felt when He claimed me, the love, compassion, and forgiveness He put in my heart, was overwhelming and intense; I was swept away, and I said to God, "I'm Yours! Do with me as You will! I'll work for You, God, for the rest of my life. Now that my son is grown and gone off to serve his country and is independent, what better things do I have to do with the remainder of my life? Nothing else is nearly as important as serving You in some capacity to help people, further Your kingdom, Lord, all to Your glory. Nothing else is meaningful for me anymore." Even that fateful day after April's hearing, before May's final one, when I accepted my fate and had to resign from my beloved job, I still trusted God and felt He was calling me to something else, greater, to His service or ministry. He used my addiction to get me to change. I recalled how one of my patrons who described herself as a prophet told me a year before that she was receiving His message for me that, "This is just a temporary training ground. Soon He will give you new missions."

The last few weeks of work, as my heart ached, wrapping things up, making copious notes to help the next librarian transition easily into the position, God began planting ideas in my head of what types of activities I would undertake during incarceration that would form the basis of my future work. In the meantime, He reassured me that He would meet my future needs. I would not go hungry or homeless. He simply did not want me to worry about what came *after* lockup. On the last day, after frantically wrapping up loose ends, saying heartfelt good-byes to sad, disappointed colleagues and even elected officials, departing on good terms with reassurances I would be welcomed back in the future if any possibility opened up, I drove home with a hurting heart. I asked God to provide me the opportunity, if He willed it, before leaving, to confide in one of the judges who especially liked me, the specific reason I was resigning, but the opportunity did not present itself. I did not feel led by the Holy Spirit to pursue it. I had only cited personal problems in my letter of resignation. My family and friends urged me to confide in him, or my boss or supervisor, to see if the position could be held for me or if they could aid me in my case, to intercede on my behalf, but I still did not feel the Holy Spirit wanting me to do so. As I drove home that final day of work, I prayed, "Father, if You will it, please provide me a way to return to that job. I was so happy there!" The immediate response I received was, "You fulfilled your purpose, and your time there is finished. Job well done!"

## JUNE 4TH: LETTER TO MY SISTER

Dear Lisa,

Day 19

Well, jail life goes on, the days fly by, I work, rest, read, write, repeat. I enjoy these women; friendly, caring, getting along well. I'm learning neat tricks where nothing goes to waste. Empty coffee bags become cookie bags. Empty cheese dip containers store cool-off packets. Cellophane wrappers from sandwiches are a lifesaver, storing food opened but not finished. Drinks are stored on the concrete floor, which stays cold even when the air is hot because this portion of the jail is underground (the roof isn't, but the floor and walls are). It's only about twenty-five years old, but it looks like it was built in the 1940s. It's crumbling. Large sheets of metal are drilled onto the walls where chunks of mortar already crumbled. Inmates built the jail, and I'm told the weather conditions were wrong for the material in the walls to set correctly. It is what it is; it could be much worse.

We are not allowed to have rubber bands, so I use ponytail holders to keep food wrappers closed. Peanut butter jars and drink bottles are reused constantly. Butterscotch candy and Atomic Fireballs create an exotic coffee drink along with a touch of hot cocoa and cappuccino powder. Peanut butter pie is made out of cereal for the crust, lemon filling from cookies, and peanut butter, of course. The hot pot has recipes where different types of food packs are heated and combined to emulate casseroles and other popular dishes.

My sixth request for a doctor visit to receive a medical special tray has resulted in a prescription for antacid. Laugh! I can't understand why it's such a big deal to substitute fake meat (soy) with bologna and hot dogs, not exactly costly foods. I won't pursue this. I'll be out in five months. Eating cheese and sausage from the commissary tides me over. Experienced inmates learn over time how to utilize everything in creative ways. I'm reminded of stories from the Great Depression when foil was rewashed and reused. We have become such a throw-away culture. I'll never forget this experience, and I will forever be a different person for it in positive ways, including being stronger. If anyone says I can't survive incarceration, they are very wrong! I'm surviving just fine, including ignoring fights and staying out of trouble. (Me, trouble? Laugh! Imagine that!)

Love you always!

Shannypoo

# CHAPTER 9

# Thursday, June 6th

## DAY 21: BARIATRIC DRINKING

I was excited to meet another bariatric patient at rec today. After conversing with Tammy and another young woman named Julie from the general population, another inmate closer to my age approached me.

"Are you Shannon?"

"Yes, ma'am."

"Did you have bariatric surgery?"

"Yes," I answered with curiosity, my interest piqued.

"I did too. Are you in for DWI?"

"Yes, you also?"

"Yes. I had a gastric bypass three years ago. Since then, I have developed an obsession with alcohol that I did not have before the surgery. Oh, I drank probably too much at times, but not obsessively, only on the weekends. I don't understand this mental obsession I have now. It's all I can think about, even now. It's all I want to do, drink."

"Yes!" I exclaimed. "Yes! Exactly. Me too. I did a lot of research into it and found out that ten to twenty percent of bariatric patients develop this alcohol obsession. The alcohol immediately hits the bloodstream due to the small stomach size with the sleeve surgery or lack of stomach with gastric bypass. Half as much hits twice as hard, creating a higher BAC twice as quickly, taking twice as long to wear off. This creates a more powerful 'brain reward' than people with normal stomachs experience, causing a mental obsession. It's like a 'high' we couldn't have achieved before surgery."

"Really? That makes sense, explains my obsession."

"What's your name?" I asked.

"Jan," she answered.

"Nice to meet you. How many DWIs do you have?"

"This is my third. Well, the first one was a DUI that happened quite a while back."

"How long are you in for?"

"Two hundred days." I was amazed at that.

"I got 335 days on DWI 2. Man, this sentencing disparity feels ridiculous. Who was your judge?"

She told me she had a different one, apparently not as strict, one with more compassion.

"Did you work?" I asked her.

"Yes," Jan replied. "I had a great job as a nurse."

"Did you have to quit because of this?" I asked, indicating our surroundings.

"Yes."

"I had to as well. I resigned from my position as a law librarian. It was a great job!"

She chuckled, finding humor in the irony of that, considering where we are. "Law librarian," she repeated, shaking her head. Then she added, "I put in for a trustee. I hope to make it soon."

"Oh, I'm sure you will. I hope you do too."

"I'm older, like you two," she said, indicating Tammy and me as Tammy was walking with us. "I want to be in a quieter environment. These young ones are far too noisy," she said, waving her hand toward the younger women walking ahead of us. "I want to be with more mature women, to get more rest and also to work to pass the time more quickly. I'm tired of sitting around doing nothing and unable to sleep with all the noise." Tammy and I nodded our heads enthusiastically.

"So what happened that you ended up in here?" I asked her. The next part of her story amazed me.

"Well, I was sitting by the pool sipping alcohol from a Yeti. I was out there all day. Later in the afternoon, my husband needed me to go to the store. I told him I didn't want to go, but he insisted, saying, 'I don't have the time, but it looks like you do!' I remember thinking, *Can't you tell I'm drinking? You know when I drink, I sit by the pool.* But I didn't want to admit to him that I was drinking. So I went and got caught."

"Me too!" I exclaimed, slack-jawed. I summarized my almost-identical story, describing how I went to Walmart when I was supposed to go to the nearby Dollar General.

"That's what I did too," Jan confirmed. "I could have gone to a closer store, but I figured I'd go to Walmart to buy wine while I was out."

"Wow," I responded. "Well, I hope you become a trustee soon. I'd like to compare more notes," I told her.

"Yes, me too," she replied. "I'm getting a divorce. My husband had been taking pictures of me when I was drinking, and I didn't know it. He sent them to my probation officer. He set me up so I would get arrested on probation violation. Our divorce will be final in July. When I get out of here, I'm leaving Texas, going back home to Savannah." At this, I felt a new rush of gratitude for my husband's loving support and patience. He never would have done that to me.

"I don't blame you," I told her. "I'm concerned about what others have said. Once you are in the system, you have a target on your back. Everyone I have spoken with here advises moving away as soon as possible. If I were not married, I'd return to Florida, where my family lives. My husband is wonderful to me, though. I love him so much."

"Oh, if I was still happily married, I'd stay too. I wouldn't recommend leaving your husband just to move out of Texas if you are happy," Jan said kindly.

Our hour of rec was up at this point. I hope she becomes a trustee quickly.

# CHAPTER 10

# Friday, June 7th

## DAY 22: SPIRITUAL WARFARE

Two new trustees joined us yesterday. The shake-up at first was a bit stressful, but things calmed down soon enough. I moved to the top bunk above Tammy, against the wall, so that Jan could have a bottom bunk. I was delighted God answered my prayer so quickly; now I have someone who can relate perfectly to my obsession with alcohol post-op and who has the same dietary requirements unmet in a Texas county jail.

The second lady, who I shall call Leah, says I look very familiar to her; she does to me too, but we cannot place each other. She told me, "Well, I used to be a waitress at IHOP," and I nodded, as that was a reasonable guess, although I cannot remember if I ate at the local IHOP. Perhaps I just remember seeing her at rec. Leah says she is a Christian and a prayer warrior, so we have five believers, although Tammy is quiet about it. Jan explained she is not a believer because "my parents shoved it down my throat so much as a child it turned me off."

I responded by assuring her, "I am not the type of Christian to do that; please do not be nervous around me."

"Don't worry about it," she said with a wave of her hand.

Last evening when I spoke with my husband, he informed me, "Even my sister is worried about and cares for you, but she wants you to know that she won't talk to you again until you apologize to her."

I hotly retorted, "Hell will freeze over first!" Naturally, this message upset me. In my mind, there is a long-standing resentment toward me I never understood. Whenever she became angry with me, sometimes with unpleasant curse words, I "groveled" at her feet, begging forgiveness for "offending" her, although I quietly disagreed that I did anything wrong toward her.

From my viewpoint, I have always been kind, respectful, and thoughtful to her. The things she resents me for are, in my humble opinion, unreasonable. I am greatly anxious about this. Tension with my mother-in-law increased as a result. She is, understandably, protective of her daughter. My husband only explains to his mother my side in conflicts with his sister when he needs to "calm Mom down" as she becomes angry with me due to her daughter's complaints. At these times, I cannot get a word in directly to defend myself.

A friend of mine recently asked me why I stand for "abuse," which, she asserted, I do not deserve. "Abuse." A light bulb turned on in my head. *Why did I not recognize it for what it was?* Of course, screaming at someone to their face and telling them to "bleep" off forever is verbal "abuse." Then I understood I was apologizing to my "abuser" for "abusing" me. There is nothing in the world I can do to *not* upset her because her issues are not truly about me. Then I recalled a book I read in the 1990s when it first came out, *The Four Agreements* by Miguel Ruiz.[39] I ordered and listened to an audio version from iTunes on my work commute earlier this year as I contemplated our situation. I fervently wish I could convince her to read it to understand the book's life-changing message, bringing her peace and happiness. However, I learned from experience such recommendations are futile. I recognize that what she truly needs is guidance from the Holy Spirit, spending time studying God's Word, which I did recommend, but this was not well received. I fear I came across sanctimoniously, not my intent at all.

As a result of our interpersonal conflicts, I avoided her company, especially after our last blowup, a consequence of my second DWI. Even if deserved, her words to me were delivered in judgmental anger, so intense it palpated in the air between us, coming across to me almost hatefully. I responded tersely, "fair enough." I struggled to control my temper to avoid speaking angry words in return that I could never take back. I refrained from saying anything else I would regret for as long as I could, which was not long. Unfortunately, my anger stewed. Soon enough, I admitted how I was feeling, which went over very poorly. She was giving me a ride somewhere. When we reached the destination, I exited her vehicle, informing her I would not be returning to it. I thanked her for the ride and asked her to please travel on as I would find an alternate way of returning home. I honestly feared losing my temper and saying regrettable things to her, perhaps uttering things I did not truly mean or imparting the truth as I see it, hurting her immeasurably.

The ensuing blowout was painful. I sobbed the rest of the day. My husband came to pick me up, greatly inconveniencing him as he was working. I imagine this is really what the expected apology is for; in her view, I disrespected her. In my view, removing myself from her company before I said anything I should not *was* respecting her. Six months passed between this explosive argument and my husband's message of her expected apology. She and I have not spoken since.

The tongue is a powerful weapon Satan uses to create dissension, hate, animosity, and pain. He uses people to attack one another.[40] Words are potent. God spoke the universe, planets, and all life into existence.[41] When we speak, we create. If we are not conscientious of our words, we can easily speak into existence hurt feelings, resentment, enmity. The old expression, "Sticks and stones may break my bones, but words can never hurt me," is untrue, save for wearing God's armor for protection. Although *The Four Agreements* is not a Christian book, it powerfully illustrates how damaging spoken words can be, not only for the receiver but for the speaker as well. Many scriptures address this and serve as a wonderful life instruction manual, as the Living Word does for our entire life, ensuring well-being, joy, and health.

After his phone call, I went to bed upset, thinking about how my sister-in-law expects me to apologize to her... for sinning? Having a difficult addiction God chose not to heal in one miraculous, instantaneous moment? Mental ill-health causing me to make irrational decisions stemming from an inebriated mind in a moment of madness? For failing to be as "perfect" as she is? I feel my pain and resentment building also toward my husband, who fails to tell his sister and mother to treat his wife at least politely if kindness is out of the question. Instead, he says, "I just deliver the message. Otherwise, I'm staying out of it." I told him, "If I treated my brother's wife that way, he would never speak to me again. He would disown me as his sister."

I pray continuously for God to help me forgive her and let it go because I know she truly does not know what she is doing.[42] I remind myself that if I cannot forgive, my Father in heaven cannot forgive me.[43] I take a deep breath and think, *I do forgive her and pray for her healing and happiness. I hurt and feel pain because I love her. I feel her pain, bitterness, and disappointment in a*

*life lacking what she desires. Please, God, bring her happiness and joy.*
I see the cycle of abuse that must have begun generations ago and the need to pray for it to end, immediately and completely, to break the generational curse. Abusers abuse because they have been abused.

Since I went to bed feeling pain and anxiety, my sleep was fraught with continuous nightmares. In a vivid dream, she screamed at me, "I hate you! I will never forgive you for the shame you brought to our family! I don't feel sorry for you at all! You deserve everything that is happening to you now!" Somehow, although I slept, I recognized Satan's attack and his lies. I had nightmares featuring dilapidated houses with missing roofs, moldy blankets, and ancient, deteriorating furniture. When I awoke, the Holy Spirit gently comforted me and pointed out that the nightmares were the devil's attacks and lies.

Meanwhile, as I slept, Leah was reading *The Insanity of God*, as Ruth had finished it. Now Leah is as glued to it as we were. Leah later told me how while she was reading, she heard me cry out in my sleep,

"Please, God, protect (unintelligible)... Jesus lay your hands on (unintelligible)... daily!" Everyone else heard me cry this out as well, and Leah asked them, "Does she do that a lot? Pray in her sleep?" To which they answered, "We never heard her do that before... not even talk in her sleep. She snores occasionally, that is all." They could tell I was sleeping deeply. The four Christian ladies freaked out, and Kristy leaped up off her bunk suddenly, stood up on one of the tables, put her hands up, and prayed eloquently over the tank, according to Leah, who said to her, "Wow, that was an amazing prayer! You're good at that!"

"I don't know where that came from, but for God. He must have been using me," replied Kristy.

"There's spiritual warfare going on in here right now!" Leah declared.

After a while, I suddenly woke up when the TV inexplicably became very loud, although no one adjusted the volume. I sat up, and the women looked at me and said, "You were just praying!"

"What?" I asked.

"You don't remember?"

"No," I answered.

Having pulled my earplugs out so I could hear them, I returned them to my ears, and sleep overtook me once again. Leah and the others described the events of the evening to me the next morning. They all asked me if I regularly pray in my sleep.

"No one has ever told me that before, so I don't think so… not that I know of, anyway."

I feel powerfully this was not a coincidence, and I also feel God urging me to write lest I forget.

# CHAPTER 11

# June 9th

## LETTER TO MY SISTER

Dear Lisa,

Day 24

I'm in good spirits. Just received your second card. I really appreciate it, especially with how busy you are. Thank you for taking the time to write; it's very encouraging, and I love having the pretty cards to look at.

I'm writing a lot, and I received a letter from my pastor—very nice. A friend from church wrote to me and came to visit me twice. I've seen Tim twice as well. No one else has come, but that's okay. I'm very blessed with all the love and support.

I was overwhelmed with the amount of gifts received last week, deeply humbled and touched. Tim sent two, and yours and Chris and Trish's arrived at the same time. The commissary lady said I broke the record. That was a first for her, and the CO on duty seemed annoyed because she had to help bring the packages in. (But she is a very nice lady, albeit quite stern; she's highly respected and compassionate all at the same time.) She was teasing me about it later. I was thrilled with the lotion, chocolate, and coffee. They are luxuries that mean the world to me because they make a difference in this harsh environment.

Thank you again for all you've done to help me. I'm expressing my gratitude to Trish and Chris too. I called Chris, and I wrote them a nice letter. I haven't called you or anyone else multiple times because of the cost. I've spent $40 on phone calls so far. Multiple ones to Tim, one to you, and others to thank them. It adds up quickly! After getting everything I need, the funds are low. Tim put $20 on so I can keep calling him because he's lonely and misses me so much (which is a good thing!). He highly values the calls. I'm talking to him an average of three to four times a week.

I spoke with Dad on the phone yesterday, and he was so sweet. Very loving, supportive, and nonjudgmental. He has really mellowed into a very loving person.

I really do believe the days will fly by, and before I know it, the end of October will arrive, and I'll be free and done with all this! Then I'll be busy with new projects, writing, and painting.

Pray for me to have strength and courage. I'm safe for now. Everything is okay.

Love you!

Shannypoo

# CHAPTER 12

# Monday, June 10th

## DAY 23: DEPARTURE

Daily, there are more changes, naturally. Leah returned after a few nights to the general population. Another girl came in and left after one hour. I called my husband Sunday evening, who finally had good news for Kristy. She had me ask him to find out her friend's phone number by tracking him down where he works. Tim did so, successfully obtained it, and I gave it to her. She successfully contacted him and finally received reliable help. He is someone from her past who is still in love with her. He told her that this current desire to help her is not based on romantic inclination but God prompting him. I hope this is true, that God is reaching out to her through her friend as He has me. I pray she continues her journey to healing and sobriety. *It's out of my hands now, Lord,* I thought. *I hope I did everything You wanted me to.* Kristy worked through *The Key to the Expected End* workbook, showing promise and sincerity. Now that her friend bailed her out, I feel happy and hopeful for Kristy, but my heart aches.

Jan is watching *Supernatural* on TV. We agree the lead character actors, Jensen Ackles and Jared Padelecki, are very good-looking.

"I used to watch this show with my son," I just told her, "when he was young, still at home. It makes me feel sad and nostalgic, and I miss my little boy." My heart swells with ache even more. All the years gone, people I love departed from my daily life or permanently... all the mistakes and bad decisions I made.

Lights are out because a nice CO is on the floor, who lets us stay in the dark to be cool and to sleep. Sad images of demons torturing humans in the TV show flash across the screen, and I feel my mood sink even lower.

Tim told me last night how depressed he is, stressed, tired, feeling hopeless. He feels tremendous pressure to pay all the bills, get the chores done, and his band ready for a gig in August. I feel so bad for him and remorseful because he is going through this for my mistakes. Thank God he still loves and supports me.

I feel a mixture of blessings and sadness. I am fighting doubts tugging at me that God will truly prosper us following these changes, with me in jail, writing, and ministering. I pray, "Please God forgive my doubts, help me with my unbelief,[44] bolster my courage and chase away my blues over a past I cannot change."

My heart aches for my mother and other loved ones who passed, and for my little boy, so sweet, precious, now a grown man with a promising future, serving his country. At least I am joyful that God watches over him. We are also blessed that my son is successful enough now to be independent, given my present circumstances. *Thank God for that!*

# CHAPTER 13

# Tuesday, June 11th

## DAY 26: BAPTISM

Ruth and I were baptized tonight, along with ten inmates from other tanks. The night was warm and pleasant. The turquoise sky was clear with a bright half-moon. The women's jail ministry brought in a brand new trough containing cold but refreshing water. They played Christian worship music, so I was thrilled to hear Toby Mac's "Love Broke Thru." I really miss listening to contemporary Christian worship pop/rock; my favorites include Toby Mac, MercyMe, Sidewalk Prophets, Hillsong, DC Talk, Crowder, Matt Redman, Danny Gokey, Mandisa, Holly Holcomb, Lauren Daigle, among many others. Who do I dislike? I love them all!

The baptism felt cleansing spiritually and refreshing physically but lacked miraculous happenstance. I did not anticipate a miracle anyway, but the female chaplain informed our group in the previous night's "baptism class" that the Holy Spirit *always* bestows the gift of speaking in tongues. Upon hearing this, Ruth and I looked at each other with an expression that says, "huh?" The chaplain was emphatic on this point. Everyone would speak in tongues. She made two more points that made us look at each other, puzzled, and later we agreed with each other that we disagreed with her. The chaplain said that eventually, God's grace runs out. After a certain period of time living in sin, He gives up, writing off the perpetual sinner. Her third point was that if any of us have anger, bitterness, or resentment in our hearts, then we are not to take communion because "Jesus deserves us at our best." Communion was given before baptism. Never in my life did I hear a priest, minister, or pastor say, "Now come forward to take communion unless you are angry today." Just the act of communion brings me peace and love, even if my heart is troubled. Jesus, in fact, included Judas at the Last Supper.[45]

No one miraculously spoke in tongues, either inmates or ministering ladies. No one prophesied either; another gift she told us would be immediately bestowed upon the freshly baptized. The chaplain said that when everyone received this gift, "speaking to others about their faith," as she defined it, "would happen next." Although this did not happen after baptism, there were many joyful smiles and hugs. We stood in a circle, joined hands, and sang MercyMe's "I Can Only Imagine" as the music emitted from a boombox brought in for the occasion. Everyone seemed to know the words to this song! The experience was happy and positive. Alex, Peni, Bahati, and Renee participated. I hugged and congratulated each of them. I wondered if Loreana would have chosen to be baptized also if she had not been released the previous week. I chose to be baptized a second time as a symbolic dedication of ministry for God, as I believe wholeheartedly that this incarceration is the beginning of a new adventure in life with God as my employer. I also choose to see it as a cleansing of my alcohol addiction.

When Ruth and I returned to the tank, I noticed Tammy crying. No one else paid attention to her. I went over to comfort her and ask what was wrong. She missed the opportunity to sign up for the baptism class because she was at court. The chaplain told her, "No." She could not be baptized because the class was required. Tammy asked the previous evening before class began if she could join in, with enough time to be pulled out of the tank. Ruth and I both asked the chaplain to do this, but she refused. She said she would ask about it later but never did. We thought it was up to her anyway. Tammy tearfully explained to me that she asked the chaplain the next day if she could also be baptized. "She not only said no, but she laughed about it rudely."

There is something edgy about this chaplain that bothers us. I encouraged Tammy to let it go, assuring her it has nothing to do with Tammy. Ruth and I shared our thoughts with her about the chaplain's teachings in the class, including the key points with which we disagree and how the chaplain's attitude and demeanor gave a cold impression. By contrast, we feel pure love and caring from the other ministers who participate in the chaplain's programs. The chaplain gave the inmates the choice of ministers to baptize them. Ruth and I chose two women in particular who are especially loving and pleasant.

This experience taught me that if God calls me into this type of ministry, I will definitely focus on emanating Jesus' light, love, and compassion, without getting "hung up" on rules or erecting unintentional barriers that discourage women in need of His loving ministrations. Ruth and I found it ironic when, during "Baptism class," the chaplain stated, "I've handpicked my ministry team because I am very particular. I don't want any of my ministers to come across as harsh or judgmental."

# CHAPTER 14

# Wednesday, June 12th

## DAY 27: THE MADNESS OF TINY STOMACH DRINKING

While Jan and I were lying on our bunks today, we talked about life, legal troubles, our charges, etc. Jan said, "I didn't know my lawyer was going to put me on the stand. I wasn't prepared for it at all," referring to her sentencing hearing.

"The same happened to me!" I said.

"And the DA came at me hard. My husband told his lawyer, who is representing him in our divorce, about an old DUI I had from the 1990s, and the DA used that to make it look like I've been a drunk forever."

"That's horrible!"

Jan continued, "My husband set me up good, installing video cameras I didn't know about, buying me wine and drinking with me, knowing I'd be on video, to have proof I was violating my probation. He also knew that every time he went out of town, I would buy alcohol, and he would have evidence as I carried wine bottles into and out of the house in order to give my probation officer evidence of my probation violation."

I described my sentencing hearing in return, "My lawyer called me on the stand without warning me ahead of time. I didn't know what to expect. We definitely weren't on the same page. He was still trying for continued probation, but it was too late for that. I had already resigned from my job, so I couldn't afford probation. Plus, if I managed to get my job back, complying with the terms of probation as he described them to the court would have been too strenuous. I'd have to drive an hour each way once a week for a UA and for probation officer visits, requiring missing several hours of work each week. Running a public library solo just made that impossible. So when the DA questioned me, I was honest because I just wanted to serve my jail time at this point and be done with it."

"Yeah, at least we will be done when our time's up; no more probation, free to go," Jan stated.

I added, "My lawyer also did not warn me that the DA was going to show the police officer's dashcam video of my arrest, which was humiliating. Three church friends were in attendance to support me, along with my husband."

"In my case," Jan contributed, "the DA gave the judge the officer's video to view privately in his chambers."

"Geez, that would have been nice," I sighed.

"I just know that I can never drink again," Jan said. "I was killing myself with alcohol."

"I don't want to go back to that madness," I agreed.

"It got bad. After a while, it was almost twenty-four seven. I started drinking in the morning. I went on binges for days, drinking and sleeping, not eating. This was after I quit working."

"I hear that!"

"I drank at work when I served food at a country club. There was a bartender who hooked me up all day. By the time I was off work, I was trashed. I always drove home with a drink in my hand. The obsession was so powerful."

"Did you ever blackout?" I asked her.

"Oh yes, all the time."

"It really helps to know I am not alone in this behavior... insanity."

"Yes. I am scared," Jan admitted. "If I ever drink again, that will be it. It will kill me. I'll get cirrhosis of the liver."

"I worry as well. I can only trust God to keep me healthy and sane as long as I am obedient to Him. I could not stay sober without Him. Honestly, I wouldn't want out right now. The temptation to drive straight to the store to buy a bottle of wine, Pinot Grigio in particular, scares me. I discovered that kind smells the least of all the wines."

"That's true!" agreed Jan. "I'd go to QuikTrip and buy a four-pack of it and a Styrofoam cup with ice. No one could tell, or very few people did. Some may have suspected."

"Yes! I did the exact same thing! I thought I was so unique and clever!"

She laughed. "No, you weren't the only one doing that."

"I got tired of not remembering the night before. Or waking up with bruises on my body or face, not remembering why, but knowing I must have fallen down. One time, the bridge of my nose hurt like mad, and my eyeglasses were cracked."

"Yeah, that was pretty much a nightly thing, passing out drunk, or blacking out, not remembering, waking up thinking, *What did I do? Am I in trouble?*"

"Oh yes! I would cringe and tiptoe in the kitchen to pour myself a cup of coffee, with Tim sitting at his computer, hoping he wouldn't ask, 'So... what *were* you drinking last night?' and I would think, *Dang it! Here we go!* feeling so humiliated, regretful, promising… what? I would never drink again? I would usually say, 'I promise not to do that today.'"

"Right!" Jan laughed. "I know exactly what you mean."

"I got caught the first time on railroad tracks. I could not remember getting there, where I was, why I was wherever I was, other than I was trying to get home."

"When I was pulled over, I knew I was cooked. I declined a field sobriety test. I just gave them my wrists and said, 'Don't bother, just take me to jail.'"

"I should have done that too. I didn't understand why the officer was bothering. It was obvious I had been drinking in the car with open, empty containers. I was completely cooperative."

"I was too. Same situation. Very messed up, open containers… hopeless situation."

"I researched this," I informed Jan, "and we are far from alone. I read similar accounts in articles and heard stories at AA meetings. Once, a woman described eerily similar circumstances where she 'came to' in her car, stuck on railroad tracks. It blew me away. She had the surgery also."

"I even drank before AA meetings. I hated them!"

"Me too," I admitted.

"Well, once again, it just helps to know this is a medical condition, a brain chemistry issue, reward-pathway with physical addiction, and a phenomenon with bariatric patients. We probably wouldn't be in jail if we never had the surgery."

"Definitely not," agreed Jan.

"That we aren't alone," I added.

"Yes. This should be discussed in your book."

"Speaking of which, I am working on it now. Perhaps I'll discuss how TDCJ deals with addiction-driven crime, especially with inmates who have health issues after bariatric surgery; this could be one of the issues highlighted."

"That's excellent. Do that! It's needed!" insisted Jan.

"I've been asking people if I can share their stories, reassuring them I will change names to protect privacy and the innocent." Jan assured me I could share her story. I was very glad to have corroboration, validation. We have so much in common.

---

Later this afternoon, I was delighted my pastor visited me. I appreciate it so much that he not only takes time to write me encouraging letters but also visits. I assured him before that I listed him as my pastor on the visitor form so that the jail would grant him the privilege of unlimited time and private visits outside of visiting hours. We met in a private, small room with closed doors, divider walls, and glass windows. Conversations are channeled through untapped phones for attorney-client privilege and privacy as they are the same rooms used for attorney visits.

Pastor reassured me I am missed at church; members worry about me and look forward to welcoming me back. He updated me on church news and asked me if I needed anything. I said that I have enough food and explained the problem with the jail meals. He asked if the church could mail me the Sunday school guides, and I answered that this was only possible if the materials were sent directly from the publisher, but books could also be sent directly from Amazon. I informed him that the chaplain gave me a Bible and study guides.

"How is the chaplain here? What do you think of him?" he asked.

"I'm glad you asked that, Pastor," I answered him. "I do have some questions for you. I was baptized last night."

"Oh really?" he asked. "That's great!"

"Yeah. I decided for the second baptism to symbolically dedicate my service to God, that henceforth He can be my full-time employer, that I'll do whatever He wants me to, whatever type of ministry He plans for me."

"That's wonderful!"

"Thank you," I smiled. "But we had to take a Baptism class, and the chaplain made a couple of points I wanted to ask you about."

"Okay," he said.

"She made the statement that at some point, 'Grace runs out,' that God gives up when He decides the sinner is never going to change."

"I would not call it 'Grace runs out,'" he answered, "not exactly, anyway. There is a scripture where God gave up on the Israelites at one point and wiped them all out to start over. If He knows someone is never going to change, He stops trying."

"Okay."

"What else?"

"She said if people have any anger in their hearts, they shouldn't take communion… that Jesus deserves us at our best."

"Well, Jesus gave communion to His twelve disciples even when one of them in His inner circle, Judas Iscariot, was a traitor, and Jesus knew this but still included Judas in communion. If Jesus didn't judge and exclude Judas in the first communion, who am I as a pastor to say a member of the congregation shouldn't take communion because of what is in his heart?"

"That is an excellent point!"

"Was there anything else?"

I thought for a few seconds, and I then remembered the lecture on speaking in tongues, which I brought up.

"Oh God," said the pastor. "Okay, well, the Holy Ghost gives many gifts, about seven, and they are not all the same for everyone, so speaking in tongues is not a mandatory thing or 'something everyone does'! One of the gifts, however, is discernment, and this is one every Christian should receive and develop. It is important to be able to discern between the true Holy Spirit and a religious spirit."

"I see," I responded. "Like you, Pastor, you have a true anointing from God. When you preach God's word, you shine God's light and emanate His love. Your sincerity is evident. If I'm uncomfortable with a religious leader who doesn't seem to be loving or something seems to be off, this is a case where discernment is helpful."

"Yes," he agreed. He then indicated that Wednesdays would be a good day to visit since he comes to Greenville anyway for Wednesday night Bible study. He asked me what he should relate to the church about me.

"Tell them I'm happy and well; I'm doing God's work to the best of my ability, testifying, witnessing, loving, encouraging, and giving hope whenever possible. Tell them I'm working on a project for God and I'm learning a tremendous amount, that I see my incarceration as part of my training ground because God is calling me into His ministry."

"My mother was stricken with polio as a young woman and was bedridden the remainder of life. But she ran a business successfully from her bed, and she also ministered from it. Countless times I saw her holding hands with others while she prayed over them. There's a poem called 'Bloom Where You Are Planted.' Mother touched countless lives right from her bed. That is what you are doing from this jail."

"I love that! Thank you so much! At work, I had a candle holder made of glass; the candle rested inside, so its light shone through the glass, illuminating flowers and the saying, 'Bloom where you are planted.'" I smiled really big.

With that, he had to get going. "See you next Wednesday!" he waved.

"Wonderful! Thanks again, Pastor!" I called as he exited the small visiting room.

# CHAPTER 15

# Friday, June 14th

## DAY 29: DREAM WEEPING

Sleep evades me this week. I am drinking too much coffee and exercising less. I am too anxious. I am dreaming vivid, crazy dreams, tossing and turning. Ruth told me about an allergy pill on the commissary list that will help me sleep. I ordered two pills on Tuesday for Thursday's delivery and tried one last night, the only night I slept soundly, like a log. Apparently, I snored all night. Ruth said it is a loud snore. Jan said I sound like a purring kitten. Other nights, they reported that I tossed, turned, kicked, knocked stuff off my "headboard," the metal rail against the wall on which I display my greeting cards, propped up by the little Bob Barker deodorants. I rest my glasses on it before going to sleep. I woke up once with my glasses on my chest; deodorants and greeting cards scattered on the floor. My tankmates said I cried and wept. I sounded truly sad, emitting miserable sounds. I cannot remember the dreams causing this. I vaguely recollect a jumbled mass of images, including car wrecks. Familiar faces pass through my dreams. I am reserving the second allergy pill for a few nights since I cannot order more until Sunday. Even though each one costs fifty cents, they may be well worth it. Hopefully, ordering five at a time will be doable.

Ruth mentioned the possibility of early release due to good behavior and overcrowding. She said there are no guarantees, but it is common enough to get bumped up from two-for-one to three-for-one to make room for new inmates. I started daydreaming of this becoming a reality, being released by August's end rather than October's. I prayed, "God, please make this a reality if it is Your will."

Ruth is set to depart for SAF-P at any time, anxious to do so. She is currently serving "dead time" in this county jail, counting for nothing because SAF-P is a set program of either six or nine months, depending on location and medical conditions. The program's effectiveness has a poor reputation with a thirteen percent success rate, according to one of the COs. Ruth claims local judges love it because they receive checks directly from the program for each inmate sentenced there.[46] So local judges do not consider other more successful alternatives such as Cenikor.[47] "It's all about the money," declared Ruth, "not about the offender's welfare or recovery." She told me that the money incentive motivates judges to sentence petty thieves to SAF-P, leading to its crowding, causing long wait times for beds to become free, even though it is an alcohol and drug recovery program. She believes that offenders will be sent to SAF-P repeatedly, although the program obviously is not helping said habitual offenders.[48]

At any rate, Ruth's anxiety is increasing daily. I pray for her sake that it happens soon, although I will miss her. She is very helping me acclimate to jail life as a trustee.

# CHAPTER 16

# June 17th

## LETTER TO MY HUSBAND

Dear Tim,

Day 32

A brief list of requests:

- Could you call Kristy's friend Miles and ask him how Kristy is doing? He bailed her out last week, and we are curious how she is.
- Solicit a donation from Dad if you haven't already.
- Send me a family picture.

Thank you!

I've been here for a month! Yay! One down, several more to go! I'll be home before you know it! Did I mention things I'll never again take for granted?

- ice
- cold drinks
- hot food
- microwave
- floss

- toothpicks
- nail clippers
- tweezers
- hairdryer
- curling iron
- makeup
- being outdoors
- a large selection of movies to watch
- knife to cut food
- fresh brewed coffee, half and half
- butter
- pain killers
- thick mattress

You are my wonderful, darling husband, who I adore so much! I love you forever and always! "Bae" is how the youth call it today, eh? You handsome man. XOXO. I appreciate you more and more every day!

Me2

PS: I count my blessings, and you are the greatest blessing in my life.

# CHAPTER 17
# Tuesday, June 18th

## DAY 33: MIDNIGHT SHAKEDOWN

I experienced my first "shakedown" after a month incarcerated. The CO, Ms. Miranda, came in just before one o'clock in the morning after turning on the lights, announcing, "All right ladies, you know what this is." I was already awake, having just stretched in an effort to relieve muscle and joint pain. I lack Ibuprofen and Tylenol, so all I can do is stretch and try yoga poses. My shoulders, upper back, and neck are in pain.

"I need you to bring me any contraband now," Ms. Miranda said, sitting at one of our tables, wearing rubber gloves and holding a trash bag. "Do this now so I don't have to put it in my report." We complied. The only contraband items I had that I knew of were rubber bands made from gloves that Ruth gave me weeks before to keep snack bags closed. She made them for her long hair because the twenty-five-cent commissary hairbands are woefully inadequate to keep her thick curls piled on top of her head, which is essential to fit under hairnets we must wear to serve food. I voluntarily submitted them following Tammy's example, who did the same.

"If you have extra books," Ms. Miranda instructed, "give them to me now." We did so. We previously hid them under our uniform tops on an unofficial library visit during our work shift. The last official library visit was three weeks ago, and we are running out of things to read. One of the nice COs let us "borrow" some. A few library books were left behind by departed inmates.

"Now nothing is left among your possessions that is contraband, right?" We affirmed that this was so. Having dressed for her as soon as we got out of bed, she said, "All right, out to the rec yard." During this time, our stuff was theoretically searched. Ms. Miranda left us outside for thirty minutes. The sky was clear with a bright, full moon. The temperature was pleasant.

My tankmates grumbled about being tired. "She will leave us out here for an hour!" they wailed. "I'm tired! I want to go back to bed, to sleep," another groaned. The litany continued.

"At least we get to see the moon," I contributed. "A full one at that. And to see the night sky, which I haven't seen in a month." I smiled at them hopefully, but they didn't look convinced that this was something about which to be positive. So I continued to stretch, trying to alleviate pain, as I admired the moon, night sky, stars, breathing in fresh air. Soon enough, Ms. Miranda returned to take us back to our tank.

I do not blame my companions for being grumpy. I am also from lack of sleep and pain. My thin mattress is taking a toll. Continuous nightmares plague me. I am losing focus on prayer. I recently read excellent books by Ruth Meyer and Max Lucado to combat depression and negativity. My thirst for more spiritual and Christian literature increases, but the lack of library visits has driven me to read *Unbroken* by Laura Hillenbrand. Ruth checked it out on her last visit. Happily, this book quickly engrossed me. The limited television programming is uninteresting.

Ruth has an allergic skin reaction to some unknown element, perhaps the clothing detergent the jail uses. She cannot obtain medical help, however, no matter what creams or other potential placebos are given her. Before the shakedown last evening, the nurse denied her request for Claritin, saying that she would have to see a doctor at a cost of twenty dollars and ten dollars for a prescription. If the issue persists, the nurse threatens to revoke her trustee status. I agree with Ruth that this is ridiculous. Her situation does not warrant two-for-one time. She is, essentially, working for the jail for free.

Jan is experiencing a similar issue. She asked for Benadryl for her allergies and was denied for an even more ludicrous reason: "Must see a psychiatrist for $40 to obtain this prescription."

Although I agreed to pay $20 for a doctor consultation regarding my diet, the visit never happened, nor was I charged for it. I submitted a request based on Ruth's advice to claim I have an "allergy" to soy to see if that would work to get protein substitutions. Instead, I was given allergy medicine of what type I do not know, but that prescription ran out. I did not argue with the COs who dispense medicine. I just took what I was told, hopefully making their job a little easier. The inmate complaints they deal with are tiresome. Based on Ruth's and Jan's experiences with medical requests, I decided to drop the matter because I cannot lose trustee status.

Meanwhile, I ceased asking for pain medication. Inmates can only get one or two Ibuprofens or Tylenols for aches and pains. When more medicine is requested, inmates must "see the doctor for $20" to obtain a prescription. Inmates are warned the $20 fee will be debited from their account upon request and will not be refunded should the visit not happen, regardless of the reason. I am grateful $20 was never debited, considering the oversight to be God's work, so I will not be rolled. The commissary allergy pills I bought were Chlorophen. Ruth told me that at state jail, inmates could purchase a thirty-count bottle for one dollar. Most items at the state commissary are much cheaper than at county commissaries. Our county contracts with Keefe.

## JUNE 18TH: LETTER TO MY HUSBAND

My dearest, most loving husband,

Day 33

I really miss eggs. Fried, scrambled, omelet; doesn't matter, just real eggs! When you pick me up upon release, can we please go to the Waffle House or IHOP?

I need stamps, envelopes, pens, and money on account for medicines (Ibuprofen and Tylenol, Chlorophen for sleep); cannot get these off the meds card.

Thank you so much! Love you always and forever. Your most devoted wife,

Me2

PS: I haven't felt like calling the past twenty-four hours. Just tired, grumpy, not sleeping well, hurt, pain head to toe and no pain killers; have to deal with it. And nightmares.

# CHAPTER 18

# Wednesday, June 19th

## DAY 34: WATER, WATER EVERYWHERE

Today I am tired and grumpy. My tankmates call me "sunshine," a nickname I earned eighteen years ago due to my "sunny" disposition; however, even sunshine has cloudy days.

The day before was Tuesday's commissary. I received the Chlorophen. I took one last night, put my earplugs in, and fell deeply asleep in no time. The respite is greatly needed after five nights of restless, broken sleep due to physical pain and continuous, vivid nightmares. Many were cataclysmic but were just a nonsensical, jumbled mess. A full night's sleep is a welcome, blessed relief. I need to pray more for protection before I sleep!

Perhaps I am grumpy partly because Ruth is still here. This means yet up to another week feeling her frustration, impatience, and yearning to be gone. Previously, I was happy for the delay, enjoying her company, learning so much from her, but after a month of her continued presence and resulting unhappiness, it is taking a toll. On the other hand, I admire how well she handles her situation overall, praying, studying her Bible while missing out on her son's wedding. I am not weary of her company or person, just her situation. I pray, "Dear heavenly Father, for my own peace and daily mind renewal, as well as Ruth's, help us focus on the positive, on our blessings, and Your purpose for our lives."

During my sweet slumber (frustrated dreams aside), we had a torrential downpour last night. For this one reason, I regret sleeping through the night as I enjoy listening to the sound of rain on the roof and rolling thunder, as long as a storm is not dangerous or tornadic.

On the other hand, every time Greenville has a hard rain, parts of the jail flood. This means trustees bring out the mops and buckets, painstakingly sopping up all the water and wringing it out into the buckets, especially when the "squeegee" is missing. This fine tool is like an extra-long windshield wiper, quickly pushing the water down the nearest drain. Every tank, thank God, has two drains, one near the toilets and one in the shower. This time we had to mop up water, the squeegee missing, more than likely carried off for use down the men's halls.

With all the money the county undoubtedly receives from commissary kickbacks and other sources, I think a few more squeegees could be purchased. The jail was built partially underground, where the women's floor is located. Continuous flooding during the rainy season, and occasional mischief on the part of the inmates who purposefully clog toilets and drains, take a toll on mold and insects. Poor construction and building design contribute to the problems. Apparently, the jail continues to meet minimum standards.[49]

# CHAPTER 19
# Thursday, June 20th

## DAY 35: DISASTER

I lived in the Pensacola area a combined total of twenty-six years. Ironically enough, when the most catastrophic hurricane hit, I was living in North Carolina. Not that I had not experienced the effects of hurricanes before; in 1995, Hurricane Opal[50] cost me a beach job, which was the worst timing, having just financed a new car; immediately thereafter, I discovered I was pregnant.

I find it ironic, after living in Texas for thirteen years, that the area near where I reside was hit by two tornadoes while jailed. We lost power for twelve hours. Air conditioning was out for several hours after the electricity was restored. The jail fared well. As far as we know, the building is undamaged. My husband joked that I was in "the safest place in the county." The jail is located near the courthouse and downtown, which was hit hard, with many downed trees that were there "forever," according to life-long residents who either work for the jail or are incarcerated in it. Many roofs are missing. The steeple of a nearby church fell into its sanctuary.[51] Tim said that Whataburger's roof partially caved in, but they still opened the next morning and served breakfast.

The inmates could not see news covering the area's damage due to local power outages. My husband delightedly told me that our boxer was on the local DFW Fox 4 News channel. He recognized him along with our house after their helicopter flew over. Tim joked that "at least you couldn't tell that he was 'doing his business.'" Tim described the area trees as "bent and twisted, if not completely uprooted." Thankfully, our house and the family property are undamaged. Tim witnessed the tornado's damage immediately after they hit the previous evening because he was in town shopping at Walmart.

During the tornadoes, our floor boss (CO) was gone for hours. We were not told anything, and after sitting in the dark without any fifteen-minute checks from the floor boss, we hit the front desk/booking intercom, asking, "Why is our floor boss missing? What is happening?" We received a stern threat: "If you use the intercom again for a 'non-emergency,' I'll write up the entire tank! Don't do it again!" We thought his response was unfair. We did not know about the tornadoes, only that there was a bad storm. Our floor boss returned four hours later.

---

Recently, Jan and Tammy were working one night when the sergeant on duty made them clean the public bathrooms and padded cells, a gruesome job involving excrement and vomit. During the bathroom cleaning, the sergeant stood over them as they were on their hands and knees scrubbing floors and toilets. As Jan cleaned a commode, the sergeant said to her, "Get it so clean that I could eat off it," laughing, humiliating her.

I was appalled hearing this. He stood over them also as they cleaned a vomit-covered padded cell, amused. Normally, male trustees are given these tough assignments. The sergeant did not offer hazmat suits or face masks, nothing aside from the regular latex gloves always used for serving food and cleaning. We pondered the humiliating treatment. Ruth said that it was abnormal, nothing she witnessed before during her many visits to this jail.

The next night they were called out at 2:30 a.m. to detail a vehicle, another odd task, especially given the time of night and one normally given to male trustees.

Within days, this same sergeant came down to the women's floor to speak with our floor boss when he spotted Jan working, and he said to her, "You look familiar; where have I seen you before?" He then named her last address she had resided with her soon-to-be ex-husband, and everything clicked into place. He was a first responder to an incident they were called to at their residence. She remembered him then as her husband's friend. He must know about their impending divorce and her husband's accusations of spousal abuse. The sergeant is clearly biased if he believes that Jan abused her husband, so his humiliating treatment makes sense.

After the recognition and confirmation that he knows her, another incident revealed his bias. She needed a notary for some paperwork. The floor boss called booking for a notary at 10 p.m., specifying that Jan was in need of it for her legal paperwork. The antagonistic sergeant happened to be on duty. He purposefully held off, we think, until 2 a.m., to come down, at which point, after staying awake hours waiting for him, Jan finally fell deeply asleep. She was made to wake up, dress fully, and go out on the floor to get her documents notarized.

Later, our floor boss agreed that there was no obvious reason for the delay because the front was not busy. I told Jan that while he probably is not breaking rules, his conduct is unprofessional, letting personal feelings cloud his judgment. Jan described the abuse *she* received at her husband's hands and how photographs of it were shown in court, which dismissed the ex-husband's charges against her.

---

I fell this week. One of the male sergeants enacted a new rule after he spotted a female inmate only wearing panties and her T-shirt as he checked tanks for our temporarily absent floor boss. He became so angry at this that he decreed all females must wear long pants, not boxers, at all times when not on their bunks. This new rule makes life harder in the summer as the tanks get very hot during the day. Only two of our floor bosses enforce it. When I need to make quick trips off my bunk at times stricter COs are on duty, I do not want to put my pants on for thirty seconds. I run back and forth in my commissary boxer shorts. One time, I needed to throw away a piece of garbage. The trash bag is located next to the shower, which someone was using. Without thinking, I ran over to it, and my feet hit the wet floor, flying out from under me. I went down hard, my head smacking the floor with a thud. Everyone turned in shock, worried about me. I popped up off the floor and declared, "I'm fine!" to their incredulity. Luckily, the incident was funny, as I was unhurt.

I am learning about interesting things inmates do creatively to pass time, entertain themselves, and make writing easier. Their ingenuity impresses me, although some of the things they create are contraband. One of their contraband items is a "cigarette" substitute, using a recipe of hot chocolate, cappuccino powder, indigent toothpaste for a minty taste, and water. I tasted their concoction and was amazed. As a past smoker, I could see why it is satisfying.

Ruth taught me how to make safety pens comfortable to hold by folding a short piece of paper appropriate to the pen's length and rolling it around the barrel. Then thread from inmate pants is wound around it and tied off at the end. No wonder pant waistbands are stitched with six to eight rows. Knowledge must have accumulated over time that inmates remove pant thread for a variety of uses. Many issued pants are partially missing thread, but the waistbands still fit, having so many stitched rows. I appreciate the pen she made for me, being comfortable and easy to write with, but the process is too tedious to be worth the effort given the little pen's life span, quickly running out of ink. Altered safety pens are also contraband, perhaps because they are stiff enough to poke someone in the eye.

The first time I watched the girls create tampons out of sanitary napkins fascinated me. They remove the pad's outer case, carefully scrape the inner stuffing, and wind the removed cover into the shape of a tampon, forming a string from excess cotton stuffing. I have no interest in making or using these, being a tedious process, and dissecting the pads wastes a great amount of material, which is discarded. Female inmates treasure them, though, detesting the "diaper" feeling of wearing thick pads.

## JUNE 20TH: LETTER TO MY HUSBAND

Hello, my darling husband,

Day 35

Could you find some bargain-priced paperbacks for me to read, shipped directly from Amazon (third party not allowed)? I immensely enjoyed reading the following three books:

- "Battlefield of the Mind" by Joyce Myers
- "Me and My Big Mouth" by Joyce Myers
- "No Wonder They Call Him Savior" by Max Lucado

If you could find other books by these authors at bargain prices or best sellers in Christian non-fiction (or pass this request on to Trish), that would be wonderful. We are not having visits to the library for more reading material.

What date is the Iron Maiden concert? Could I get a copy of the lyrics to "Rime of the Ancient Mariner"?

Thank you so much!

Me2

PS: I also am reading Laura Hillenbrand's "Unbroken," now a blockbuster movie and a true WWII story. It's wonderful! We must rent and watch it together sometime. Can you believe it's making me interested in the history of WWII? You are the most wonderful husband in the world! I miss you, baby!

# CHAPTER 20

# June 23rd

## LETTER TO MY SISTER

Dear Lisa,

Day 38

Sorry I haven't been able to call again. Each fifteen-minute call is $3, which isn't bad, but as much as Tim needs me to call because he misses me so much, it adds up, and he isn't able to put much on my account. His mom is helping him with groceries and is working with him regarding the rent, bless her. He has doubled the number of jobs he is doing to make ends meet. He's very tired.

Gifts from others, including Trish, keep me eating and also in luxuries like chocolate, yummm, and coffee. I'm so eternally grateful for all the love and support.

My in-laws are very unhappy. I can't blame them, but I think they are confiding feelings about me to the pastor and others at church to make sure others understand "their side." I'm not worried the church will stop supporting me because I receive letters of encouragement from the members, with clear assurances that I will be welcome back after I get out, telling me I am missed. But I hear about my in-laws' doubts about me, how I'll be after I get out, both from Tim and from some at church, and it is upsetting. For this reason, my mood has been considerably low. I need a second wind of positivity. I'm experiencing such anxiety now. Even more after hearing about their doubts about my ability, or lack thereof, to recover.

What if they're right? How will life be living next door if they continue to believe the worst? How will I cope with it? How do I overcome their negative perception and trust that God has this and things will turn out fine? Tim will never move. He's dedicated to being there for them, plus he put a lot of money into the band hall. He's blessed to have bandmates with exceptional talent, and I know they will get gigs and do well. I'm lucky that Tim is equally supportive of my plans with the book and art as I am his band. I have his total support, belief, and encouragement. He has mine as well. Whether things work out with his family remains to be seen, and it scares me.

Having depression and anxiety today, my first really bad day, on the verge of tears, I had to write and share with you. I hope and pray for a solution where I can stay with my husband and find peace with his family.

There's too much estrogen in this tank with five other women, and I do love each of them, but the hourly drama, OMG, over minor stuff! It could be far worse, though. At least there are no screaming matches and claws out! Fights are far worse in the general population.

I received a loving, encouraging letter from Dad, who expresses his faith in my future work and projects for God.

OMG! I received your birthday card just now! Thank you so much! Sounds like my letter was much the same as this one. LOL. Well, at least there are a few developments. Hopefully, it is not too boring or repetitive! My spirits are considerably better now. Thank you again so much.

BTW, the phone system's still down from the storm. Somehow I was able to talk to Tim for a limited time, long enough for him to tell me bad news about their feelings regarding me, and the time ran out, so I can't even respond with how I feel about it.

Okay, it's late, time for bed! Love you. XOXO,

Shannypoo

PS: I like the picture on the card. The sepia color is cool!

PPS: I could use more stamps; if you throw in any cheese bars, I wouldn't mind!

# CHAPTER 21

# Monday, June 24th

## DAY 39: THE DAILY BUMP

The days fly by and blur into each other with repetition. Two new girls came in, but one of the two rolled herself out quickly. She said that the tank was far too serious for her. She is only twenty. She longed to be with her friends in another tank. I like her though, as she is very sweet. She is also stunningly beautiful, reminding me of Jennifer Lawrence, the actress from the Hunger Games movies. So I will call her Jennifer. She has blonde curly hair, vivid blue eyes, and a slim figure. Sadly, she faces many years potentially in TDCJ, having four felonies and impending drug-related charges. The drug epidemic destroys so many lives, wasting the potential of victims and perpetrators alike. While not the most educated, these women are intelligent. I encouraged Jennifer to see the positive in her future by turning to God and remembering that He can move mountains. I suggested she could help other women like herself in the future.

The other new trustee is named Brigitte, although I call her "Bebe." She is twenty-seven, very pretty, with blue eyes, long, curly, auburn hair, and a petite figure. She lacks teeth, as do many from using dope, which takes a great toll on oral health, especially for those who smoke it versus injection, I am told. Kristy, Ruth, Tammy, and Bahati have similar dental conditions. Bebe has a sweet personality, and I adore her. I feel like a mother hen. I enjoy speaking with her since she is opening up to Christianity and is thirsty for knowledge and reading material. She says she is ready to change direction in life, tired from the ravages of drug abuse and addiction. I suggested she read *The Key to the Expected End*, and since the chaplain just left for a two-week vacation, I gave Bebe my copy of the workbook. I can get a replacement later. I was reluctant to let my copy go, but she asked for it, and I cannot deny her. I am happy she is excited to work through it.

Bebe has a great sense of humor, bringing sorely missed laughter back into the tank. I hit my head on my bunk's "lip," which is a portion of metal on the top bunk that bends down by two inches on the right side, which is the correct one to enter and exit the lower bunk. This poor design quickly teaches new inmates to duck, but I am a slow learner, apparently. Consequently, when Bebe heard the "thunk," she looked at me and, realizing what happened, asked, "Are you okay?"

To which I replied, "I'm okay! It's just the 'daily bump.'"

At this, all the women burst out laughing, hard and long. They find my statements hysterical. "What is it? What's so funny?" I demanded.

With gasps from laughing hard, they tearfully explained, "That's what the dope shot, or 'shooting up,' is called, 'the bump.' Don't ever say that! You are so clueless about the drug world!"

Hearing this, I laughed too. Many times I reveal my naivete about drug use, manufacturing, sales, life on the street, etc. This is one humorous example.

# CHAPTER 22

# June 25th

## LETTER TO MY SISTER

Dear Lisa,

Day 40

I just received another card from you. Thank you so much! I love the picture of you comforting me when I broke my arm as a child.

I am pretty down. I'm sure you got my letter from yesterday, maybe even just now with this one, explaining why. I fear how hard it will be after I get out, return home, will be stuck without a DL, under the control of others, without any escape. I've never done well with being controlled. I fear my own rebelliousness. I fear being at the mercy of others and how they'll treat me.

I fear the debts I can't pay. All I can do is give them to God. In time, they'll get paid. I must pray more and be faithful. I wish insurance called "in case you get incarcerated." LOL.

I'm sorry I'm not upbeat. Thinking of being gossiped about at church really bothers me. I know I shouldn't let it. I don't think it's changing anyone's mind among those who love, support, and believe in me…

I still believe God wants me to write the book, and He will ensure it is published, will be a success, and financial blessings will follow. I must have faith, think positive... I can't cope otherwise.

Love you bunches! XOXO,

Shannypoo

# CHAPTER 23

# Friday, June 28th

## DAY 43: BIRTHDAY VISIT

The day that marked half a century of life is ironic in that I am incarcerated, a criminal. I think, *Well, I avoided jail for forty-nine years, could be worse!* When I was younger, I never dreamed that I would ever be jailed.

A few years ago, I conversed with someone I disliked; when she said to me, "At some point, we all spend time in jail," I protested, "I haven't! Nor will I ever!" She vexed me, but that is a whole other story. Anyway, famous last words! In fact, about a year or two ago, I heard Wendy Williams make a similar statement, and I remember thinking the same thing. I was quick to judge! *Is this one reason I ended up in jail?* I wonder. *Because of my pride?*

My birthday began wonderfully. My son visited me all the way from Hawaii. Tim joined him. The jail allowed us extra time since my son lives so far away. We enjoyed our conversation; their visit was a perfect gift. My pastor also visited. With all the love and support of family, friends, and church, I feel so blessed! My tankmates lack such a network. They each have one or two on the outside, but not the level that I enjoy. I count this blessing, thanking God continuously for it!

This evening I received many birthday cards, including those from church members who I met but cannot place a face to name. One of my great faults, I take forever to remember a person's name. I am humbled and gratified as I am when I receive commissary gift packages.

Unfortunately, my birthday ended badly. A CO rolled Bebe for passing a kite (note) to another tank after being warned from a previous incursion. She ignored the guard's warning, who now said, "I'm having none of that," immediately rolling her.

# CHAPTER 24

# Monday, July 1st

## DAY 46: DISSENSION

The night of my birthday brought hostilities, which plagued us for twenty-four hours. True, Bebe flouted the rules by passing kites, but my tankmates contradicted one another regarding who encouraged her and who set her up, only to rat her out to the guard. Fingers pointed everywhere behind backs. Possibly all of them are lying. They blindsided me, as I was oblivious to my environment, reading Steven Furtick's *Unqualified*.

Ironically, I felt "unqualified" in the heated arguments as a Christian trying to shine His light to inspire others with His love. I was frustrated, angry, and tired. The dissension drained me, so I let my guard down. I forgot to put on my armor of God, as Paul describes in Ephesians.[52] I failed as an arbitrator, mediator, and peacemaker. Although I kept my words positive about each of them to avoid gossip and backstabbing, I am imperfect, not saintly. I am failing to pass a difficult test because I conveyed my resentment at Bebe's being rolled.

Ruth and Tammy are at war. Originally, they got on well together. I cannot tell who Jan "sides" with as she vacillates between the two. I try to convince them all to embrace one another, insisting each of them are worthwhile, lovely, precious women whom Jesus loves. We are mature, adult women. We do not need to quibble over trivial matters. What a terrible twenty-four hours!

Amazingly, everything returned to "normal" Saturday evening, and the remaining weekend rolled smoothly by.

# CHAPTER 25

# Tuesday, July 2nd

## DAY 47: FULL HOUSE

The rule about daily, frequent changes was held when four new trustees joined our tank. At first, the news filled us with dread and threw us into a panic. With eight in the tank, we have a full house. We scrambled to clear off the top bunks. Our commissary orders were just delivered this morning, so we went into overdrive discussing how to protect our goods from possible theft as well as persistent begging. I love sharing but cannot to my own detriment.

However, as the evening progressed, interactions revealed a positive mix with conversation, laughter, no begging or arguing. I am cautiously relieved.

# CHAPTER 26

# Wednesday, July 3rd

## DAY 48: PULLED

On Tuesday evening, each trustee trained the new ones, taking turns each shift. Everyone got along, blessedly, and the day went smoothly.

In the wee hours of Wednesday morning, at 2 a.m., Ruth's anxious dream came true. State inmate transport came to take her to SAF-P. She "pulled chain." The intercom buzzed, calling her last name several times, rousing us from deep sleep; we failed to grasp at first what was happening. Then our floor boss came in and rushed Ruth to "pack up!" I felt bad for her; she had little time to gather what she meant to take. Consequently, she left her *Life Recovery Bible* behind.[53] Tammy spotted it and immediately claimed it. I am elated and relieved for Ruth. Since the state took so long to pull her, she was irritable for a long time, putting us on edge while fueling a feud with Tammy.

We spent the early morning hours shifting bunks. I transferred to Ruth's; Jan to mine. Maye, an older woman among the new trustees, switched to the first bottom bunk Jan vacated that I initially occupied. Thus, we rotated by seniority toward the inner wall, which reflects an ideally maintained temperature. I worry, though, about the mold on it in the corner, where water leaks down occasionally during heavy rain. Since Maye is the oldest of the newbies, she occupies the bottom bunk. Happily, the younger women politely and respectfully defer to her age.

We returned to sleep at 3 a.m., but I awoke at five o'clock, and Maye got up with me, so I snagged her to serve breakfast trays and clean with me. Since we get on well, training her is easy. In the afternoon, we conversed pleasantly, getting to know each other. I described my diet, explaining why I cannot eat much from the trays.

"But soy is good for you," she responded.

"Recent studies indicate the contrary," I answered. "At least as a bariatric patient, it is too starchy." During these moments, I missed my iPhone with instant ability to retrieve research.

"I didn't know that. I had a gastric bypass ten years ago," she contributed.

"Really?" I asked. "Did you experience addiction to alcohol?"

"No," she answered.

"That's good!" I said.

"But I've had problems recently," she added. "I'm very poor, unemployed, hungry, homeless, and live in bad places, like the one where I was just arrested, a known crack house, not that I knew that ahead of time. I don't 'use,' but I was there. I was charged with under a gram, although I did not possess any drugs. Going hungry, my body is in starvation mode. Currently, I weigh 170, but I should weigh a little bit more, being over six feet tall."

I observed her then and noticed a grayish pallor to her skin and hollowness of her cheeks, with dark circles around her eyes. My heart broke for her.

"What is your age?" I asked (by habit, I avoid the word "old").

"Thirty-seven."

"When you get out of here, what happens next?" I asked. "Will you be able to escape Quinlan for a safer place?" She mentioned living in Quinlan previously, a well-known "crack town."

"Yes, I have a gentleman friend who is helping me. He bought me groceries. He will help me move."

"Great! Get out of there as soon as possible," I sagely advised. She described her lack of family as a safety net.

"Well, I'm tired now. I'm going to nap," she said.

"Certainly. I hope we can continue to talk later," I responded.

Before this conversation, while we waited to be called out to work, we briefly talked about faith. She indicated a desire to draw closer to God to get on a better path. I was on the verge of asking if she wanted to pray together when the CO buzzed open our door. Our chance to talk later this afternoon didn't come, much to my regret. The nurse pulled her out for blood work. She returned for an hour, then our floor boss came for her, handcuffed her, and said, "You have a visitor." Maye looked happy as she left. She has not yet returned.

# CHAPTER 27

# Thursday, July 4th

## DAY 49: MISSING

The Fourth of July has been sad for those of us locked up, but we made the best of it, despite becoming emotional, missing family cookouts and fireworks. We enjoyed Macy's 4th of July Spectacular on NBC,[54] however, with patriotic music during a phenomenal fireworks display. We sang along with the national anthem, "America the Beautiful," etc., and hugged and cheered each other up. Tension of the previous week evaporated.

We worry about Maye, taking turns guessing what happened to her. Her basket of items still sits on her bunk, so we think surely, she is going to return since they haven't taken her stuff away. We wonder if she is in the hospital. This seems to be the most likely scenario since she had blood tests, but we also theorize that she is being interrogated at length about some larger criminal activity, not necessarily on her part, but possibly about a drug ring that the Sheriff's Office is trying to bust. Illegal drugs are pervasive throughout the county but concentrated in Quinlan and on Lake Tawakoni, so this scenario seems plausible.

# CHAPTER 28

# Saturday, July 6th

## DAY 51: OVERCOMERS

Friday passed uneventfully. I concentrated on reading *The Case for Christ*, Billy Graham's 1998 special edition, wherein Lee Strobel reopens his investigation into proposed theories about Jesus not being the Son of God.[55] He interviews experts in this research-dense, interview-based, academic book, which follows up his 1981 work of the same title. His original work focused on document research, so the interview-based chapters in this edition are a new format,[56] including study questions. I spent two weeks reading a bit at a time while slowly digesting the information. The book is excellent. I learned many historical facts. Archaeological evidence supports Jesus being the Son of God incarnate.

When I was not reading, Jan and I discussed our addiction, admitting to each other how difficult it is to think about drinking without feeling cravings. She informed me that she could not recall her dreams when I described my nightly dreams of consuming wine with accompanying nightmares of bad car accidents. We agree we have to fight the desire for alcohol upon release. Jan, Tammy, and I are studying together for the Overcomer's class, which is going well. The chaplain is teaching it and doing a great job. My opinion of her is improving.

# CHAPTER 29

# Sunday, July 7th

## DAY 52: MEDICAL ROLL

Maye returned today at 1 p.m., just as visitor hours began. She had several blood transfusions. The hospital just released her. She looks better with healthier skin color. We feel relieved and happy to see her. I wanted to speak with her, but I was called for a visit immediately after she arrived. When I returned, she had been rolled for health issues. The doctors failed to locate an internal leak, so she has to be closely monitored. I regret that we were unable to further our conversation since she indicated a desire to receive Jesus. We were interrupted twice before, and another opportunity to pray together eluded us.

# CHAPTER 30
# Wednesday, July 10th

## DAY 55: BAD MEDICINE
## AND LEGAL REPRESENTATION

This week is peaceful. Three younger trustees troupe through the days cheerfully. The three older ones, including me, are depressed. I pray fervently, asking the Holy Spirit for comfort, for God to chase away dark forces, to protect me and everyone else in our tank. I ask for help to stay "up." I agree with Jan that it was easier to sleep these days, spending more time escaping the blues, helping time pass by faster.

Jan suffers from a bad toothache. We still cannot obtain Tylenol because of the required doctor consultation. She wants to see the dentist, using her dental insurance to treat a tooth rather than having it pulled, but was informed, per the handbook rules, that he can only pull teeth. He has a bad reputation for painful work, lacking compassion. Jan heard the medicine dispensing CO discuss how the dentist pulled a male inmate's tooth last week, leaving half of it in his mouth and in a great deal of pain. The dentist also costs $20.00. The handbook, sadly, is out-of-date, citing the dental cost as $5 per pulled tooth. Tammy had to pay $40.00 for two pulled teeth. She told us that the dentist barely numbed her before yanking them out. She returned in miserable pain with only three days of Tylenol. I wonder if this situation with the dentist is by design as part of inmate punishment. I still hear a chorus of voices from family members and friends reciting the mantra, "Well, it is jail, what do you expect?" noticeably lacking compassion. I thought, *What is the line from normal to cruel and unusual punishment?* Granted, inmate experiences here are nothing compared to brutal jails in third-world countries, but does that justify the conditions considered less than par for US jails?

Jan conversed by phone with her sister, who told her that her husband stayed out of jail through four DWIs and probation violation. His upcoming punishment is having a breathalyzer installed on his vehicle. This reminds me of two recent examples of how my judge punished two young men with time served on DWI 3 and fines, giving light sentences compared to mine. Granted, Jan's brother-in-law resides in a different state.

Jan and Tammy have the same lawyer and difficulty consulting him. Jan's family hired him for both her civil divorce case and criminal conviction. He is Tammy's attorney by court appointment and is unresponsive to both women. They cannot contact him by phone to ask questions or to voice wishes for their cases. He blocks all calls from the jail. He never answers Jan's letters and her other attempts to communicate with him via her family. Jan most urgently wants to waive her right to appear at her final divorce hearing, which would humiliate her but be triumphant for her ex-husband, who would gloat, she fears, to see her shackled in her "pinks" (jailed-issued clothing). Her lawyer, she feels, is completely uncooperative. Similarly, for Tammy, the lawyer is typically unavailable, uncommunicative, and unwilling to advocate possibilities to lessen her sentence. Even if the ladies are wrong about him, he could assuage their qualms with regular communication. I recall the many complaints I received from inmates in their requests I serviced on my last job. Their court-appointed attorneys rarely, if ever, visited them or otherwise communicated with them. The first time they saw their legal representatives was in their court hearings.

## JULY 10TH: LETTER TO MY HUSBAND

My adorable, darling, loving husband,

Day 55

I miss you so much! I love you with every breath in my body, every beat of my heart. I miss you almost as much as I miss Ellis! Haha.

I have lots of anxiety for when I return home and have to face the disappointment and disapproval of your family. My thoughts are torturing me. Don't get me wrong, I love them and forgive all negative comments about me. I still worry about my ability to cope with negativity. I am praying for peace.

I am getting really fit. The exercise routine is working great. I'm thinner, fitter, stronger, more toned and muscular; I hurt less, have more energy, except at night—I still conk out by 9 p.m.! I am sleeping better as well.

I am still writing, reading, thinking, praying, sleeping. The Overcomers group is going well.

I look forward to getting out and eating real eggs, beef, drinking filtered ice water, and giving you a bunch of kisses. I look forward to soaking in a hot bubble bath and cuddling on the couch with Ellis while eating popcorn soaked in tons of butter and watching great movies I missed while incarcerated that become available for rental or streaming.

When I get out, I only want to see you and our fur babies for a few days. I mean this whole sincerely. No surprises! No parties! Not for two or three days, okay? Thanks. Love ya a billion times over for all of infinity, my precious husband.

Me2

# CHAPTER 31

# July 11th

## LETTER TO MY HUSBAND

My dearest, sweetest husband,

Day 56

You are the best husband in the world! The most supportive, loving. I miss you so much! My love for you is endless. I just can't wait to come home to you. I miss your sweet kisses and your bright blue eyes, your great sense of humor. You make me laugh every day. You always brighten my day, no matter how gloomy I feel. I'm glad you miss me too. Wouldn't be good news for either one of us if you didn't!

Now we are up to 160 laps around the tank! We added two hundred jumping jacks to squats as well as push-ups, lunges, obliques. I can't believe I can do so many jumping jacks! I have so much energy! I am sleeping better and feel less physical pain. Definition is forming in my leg muscles, especially my thighs and arms, which are thinner too. So is my face, but that's showing twice as many wrinkles with less fat! Squats have helped with glutes and thighs. The major problem area remaining is my belly! Belly fat is so difficult to lose!

I cannot wait to give you bunches of kisses and lay my head in the crook of your arm while holding you while we sleep.

Just wanted to send you my kisses and all my love. You can share them with Ellis, DeeOGee, Rocco, and Bangles!

Love you more than you realize,

Me2

PS: The kind of love we have makes us the luckiest people.

# CHAPTER 32

# July 12th

## LETTER TO MY HUSBAND

My dearest Tim,

Day 57

Please do not tire of me writing to you. This is the equivalent of you talking to me on the phone nightly. You need someone who loves you dearly to just listen, and I do my best to be that person for you. So letter writing is like me writing you daily notes before I leave for work in the morning, a chance to express to you my current thoughts, just to have someone I love listen to me.

What is on my mind this Friday morning at 8:10 are the horrific nightmares I'm having. I only remember some, but they make me shout out loudly, waking my tankmates. This morning's was especially bad because I woke up myself and the others shouting. A gang of men took over a women's restroom, which was full, to the point of having a waiting line, and I was in the end stall. Several men broke the stall door and piled on top of me, and I woke up sleep screaming, "Get the [bleep] off me!"

A month ago, I woke up shouting, "God, please protect me!" Last week I sleep screamed, "Lord, I hate them!" Many times I moan as if in great pain, tossing, turning, struggling against something while uttering unintelligible dribble. I pray constantly. There is true spiritual warfare going on in here, and those of us who are into Jesus are being attacked the most.

Thank you for listening. I wish I was home, and you could just hold me and protect me.

Love forever, for infinity,

Me2

## JULY 12TH: LETTER TO MY SISTER

Dear Lisa,

Day 57

Got your letter yesterday. Thank you very much. I'm sorry one of my letters went missing. Perhaps it was mistakenly tossed. In it, I basically described the negative things I heard being said about me at church, and I was pretty upset. I received loving, encouraging letters from the congregation, with reassurances I would be welcomed back. I was bummed out when I heard that a letter I wrote to the pastor was difficult to read because of my "bad" handwriting, so I'm printing this letter and letters to others just in case it is true. If my handwriting is difficult to read, please let me know. I described my anxiety regarding Tim's family, but things are getting better there.

I would love to come and visit you in the UK someday. Hopefully, my book will be published, and I'll have the financial sustenance to do so. We would have so much fun. The exercise routine has made me fit. I could go on those long hikes with you!

I'm still reading, sleeping frequently, writing, meeting more women, learning their stories. I love them all. I care about them deeply, which confirms that I need to go into some kind of ministry to help those in need.

Thank you for everything so much again. It's wonderful to be able to write and send letters, make phone calls, eat real meat, and drink coffee to help me wake up and be alert for the morning shift. I couldn't do this without your help and that from Chris, Trish, and Tim.

I'll close now. I cannot think of anything else at the moment, except that the "Overcomers" group is going well, and the tank has nice women now, so things are peaceful.

Love ya always!

Shannypoo

# CHAPTER 33

# Sunday, July 14th

## DAY 59: ENCOURAGEMENT

One of the young women, Chanel, whom I enjoyed getting to know, just rolled herself, adding to my blues. She is talented as a hairstylist, including hair braiding and threading eyebrows. I never had my eyebrows threaded before and am super impressed with the result. They never looked so nice. She is quite skilled. She braided my super short hair, which stayed in place, quite an accomplishment. Chanel has a gentle touch and a kind nature. She loves to exercise; we took up a routine twice a day. She lengthened it, making it more challenging, increasing reps and laps. My body is stronger and leaner in an amazingly short time. Unfortunately, she was bored, longing to be with her friends in another tank.

This morning I worked with another young woman who is feisty and funny. She has a positive outlook on life. She describes herself as "bad," saying she knows it and "always will be," but makes no apologies. However, she believes in God and Jesus, and she says despite her mistakes, she has no doubt she is going to heaven. At thirty-six, she is a habitual offender. I like her, though. She makes me laugh. She encourages me. She tells me to not be so down on myself or let anyone else make me feel down. "You're better than that, Shannon. Don't you put your chin down and stare at the floor all the time. Be confident. Make eye contact. You have nothing to be ashamed about. Shame on anyone else who makes you feel ashamed of yourself." She refers to how I act during our work shifts together.

"But when Ruth trained me, she emphasized being submissive, deferential, told me to look at the floor and not make eye contact with the guards," I protested.

"Well, she was wrong," insisted Lopez. I call her Lopez, as she reminds me of Jennifer Lopez. "The guards are not going to respect you, and they will be harder on you if you won't meet their eye." I shared my trepidation about the stricter guards. I think she is right. Ruth said that Ms. Connor thought it odd that I never looked at her directly, but honestly, Ruth had me scared to do so. Perhaps that is why Ms. Connor enjoys giving me a hard time. I will take Lopez's advice. Lopez's testimony is powerful. She is uplifting, enthusiastic, always bright, happy, and comforting. She prays about her most recent charges being dropped, fully believing they will be, and, when they are, will give God the credit. She has full faith in Him that they will be.

# CHAPTER 34

# Monday, July 15th

## DAY 60: TOILET PAPER DEBACLE

Jan received positive news this morning. Her lawyer is working on getting her released earlier than two-for-one time, which would be around the end of August without intercession. Her divorce hearing is scheduled Friday, July 26th. He wants her to be released in conjunction with the proceeding as part of the settlement. She is restraining herself from excitement, dreading the letdown should he fail, but she is hopeful. We are excited for her.

I was unhappy this morning because three of us had problems this week, resulting in a toilet paper shortage. Two of my tankmates are constipated, which is common in jail, and are taking medication. I had this problem in May and June, but this time I have a stomach bug producing the opposite effect. This has caused a conflict with Tammy, who fears running out of commissary supplies, especially toilet paper. When she noticed our supply is precariously low, she began hoarding tank rolls distributed for everyone's use. Unless toilet paper is purchased from the commissary, no one is supposed to keep it from others. We are all given one roll each "plus one" twice weekly. Tammy, however, is not sharing "her roll." By Sunday, she possessed the only remaining roll. She blames everyone else for running out, claiming we use too much. Truthfully, this is the first week all summer we find ourselves in this predicament because three of us are "going" far more than normal, Tammy included, for the reasons indicated. She consumed two bottles of medication, so her TP use is as much, if not more, than the rest of ours.

We ran out last night before I needed some. I asked Tammy to share. She answered, "You can use your hands. All of you can use your hands. I don't care. You can't have any of mine."

My temper intensely exploded. I am appalled that any woman would let others around her have to take such desperate measures, especially since we all are so good to her, sharing our commissary in her lean times, despite the fact that she hoards what she has. Desperately, I pounded on the window to ask for a roll. Unfortunately, Ms. Connor was on duty. When she heard my question, she yelled, "Absolutely not!" I was aghast. I could not believe the cruel denial. I burst into tears.

To make matters worse, when the COs changed shift, Ms. Connor demanded of the next one coming on duty, Ms. Miranda, "Under no circumstances is 357 (our tank number) to get any toilet paper!" After she left, Jan was working the evening shift. Ms. Miranda witnessed me crying on the phone during her fifteen-minute check. She asked Jan why I was upset, and she informed Ms. Miranda of the situation. Ms. Miranda compassionately gave me one roll. I thanked God for interceding with her. After this incident, I consulted the inmate handbook, which states on page two that "toilet paper will always be available."

This incident began an intense rift with Tammy, not just between myself and her but with others as well. Tammy's relationships are rapidly deteriorating now. I remain grateful for Lopez's comfort and encouragement, especially her advice about dealing with Ms. Connor, to not let her bully me and get me down. Ms. Connor put me in tears on a number of occasions. Lopez said, "Remember not all cops, peace officers, or COs are 'good guys.' Are you familiar with the Gary Stroud case?"

"No," I answered.

"Look it up when you get out. He was a peace officer who killed his wife. He's serving sixteen to life in prison for it."[57] I said that I would (referenced in endnote below).

Lopez is very angry with Tammy over her transgression. She told me, "When she goes to state or SAF-P, wherever she goes, with an attitude like that, she will be an SOS to the others."

"What do you mean by 'SOS'?" I asked her.

"Smash-on-sight," replied Lopez. "She's going to get the [bleep] beat out of her." God forgive me for not feeling bad hearing this.

I also stressed over a new trustee, Phoebe, when Tammy picked on her viciously, and everyone else joined in on the bullying. To credit the girl, she is "like a duck," letting it roll off her back. I apologized to her on behalf of the others when they were out of earshot, and she said innocently, "Oh, that's okay, I think they are really nice." I looked at her incredulously. Then I smiled. At least she doesn't let anything bother her. She is very sweet. I am going out of my way to treat her kindly.

Another young lady, whom I will call Miriam, also comforted me, although she is more reserved and quiet, mostly keeping to herself. She enjoys reading Christian literature, as much as she can get her hands on; we swap books, comparing notes on them. Miriam is also disturbed by Tammy's behavior.

# CHAPTER 35

# July 19th

## LETTER TO MY HUSBAND

Dearest Tim,

Day 64

A nice lady in my tank gave this picture to me, asking if I'd like to send it to you, and I said, "Yes!" I send this sweet, kissable puppy with a rose in its mouth to you with all my love. I miss you terribly. I'm so homesick! I'm done! I'm ready! I've learned my lesson! I'd never chance coming here again. I've served my debt to society. Can I come home now? LOL! XOXOXO. So post this puppy where you can see it every day to remind you how much I love you and that the flame burns eternally. I feel bad for all I've put you through. But you stand by me, and I owe you everything.

By the way, I'm low on stamps, envelopes, and money for phone calls. Otherwise, I'm good. All stocked up.

Love you eternally,

Me2

# CHAPTER 36

# Saturday, July 20th

## DAY 65: GOD'S HUG

After a month of "the blues," I woke up this morning feeling positive, with gentle reminders of how this time has deepened my walk with God and my understanding of His ways, why He created us, how He longs for our companionship, but being a just God, gives us free will to choose how we live. He did not create slaves to bow down to Him in worship. Where would be the joy knowing that if your "loyal subjects" figured out they were really slaves, they could run away at any time and might choose to do so? I finally understand this whole "worship thing." Before, I questioned why an intelligent, loving God would *want* to be worshiped? Well, it is not worship itself, but the expression of happiness, joy, gratitude that He created us, *gave* us life, free will on how to live, and despite our ability to walk away, *choose* to stay, love, seek and keep companionship with Him…that we *want* to hang out with Him, sing, dance, and have a great time.[58] He does not want programmed bots or unwilling people forced to bow down to Him for company. A loving and just God does not revel in forced devotion, but rather He wants communion with us where we acknowledge Him as our supreme Creator and give Him our thanks freely.

God stopping me gave me the opportunity to rest, sleep, contemplate, read, study, write and heal. I cannot credit the Texas justice system. All the credit goes to God, although He allows every institution to function the way it does. Every decision a judge makes is part of God's plan.[59] Whatever we go through, God wants us to stop, observe, listen, and learn. He is in control, always. His gentle reminder comforted me after feeling anguish for several weeks. My appreciation has deepened for everything I receive, big things like a great job, tiny things like ice cubes, cold water, nail clippers, fresh food served hot, salad, uncooked vegetables with dip, fresh air, sunshine, a cool breeze, a pet's love... and bigger things, like freedom! Daydreaming of being home, going outside as I please... This may seem trivial to anyone who has not been jailed, whether by the justice system, an abusive spouse, or a disabled body... Indeed, it *is* the trials and tribulations of life that give us the opportunity and desire to seek God, know Him, feel His love, comfort with a real, true, deep appreciation for His gifts.

If He didn't stop my self-destruction, I would be cracking under the pressure of my addiction, my need to be everything to everyone. I neglected rest, healing, spiritual reflection to deepen my understanding of God and the benefits of a relationship with Him. I would not have read Joyce Meyers, Lee Strobel, Billy Graham, T. D. Jakes, Max Lucado, and others, as well as additional Bible studies, daily devotionals, and the Life Recovery Bible. I would not have met some wonderful women, albeit "criminals" like myself, who ended up incarcerated as a result of their addictions and brokenness.

I woke up visualizing release... walking free out the front door, feeling the sunshine on my face... getting in my car and feeling the luxury of its leather trim seats, turning on the radio to listen to my favorite modern Christian worship music, which teaches me how to worship God joyfully and provides the opportunity to hear the Bible lyrically. I fantasize arriving home to watch my favorite TV shows, to see fireworks in person… to hold my husband's hand, gaze into his pretty blue eyes and see his love for me there, to laugh at his jokes as he entertains me with his wit and wisdom… to greet my dogs and bask in their love and joy as they see me for the first time in months, and to patiently pet each of them as they compete for attention, jumping on me, knocking each other over to be the first to give kisses. To go into my house and drink hot, fresh-brewed coffee with real half-in-half and enjoy a real meal of fried eggs with runny yolks and bacon, or a juicy hamburger made with real one hundred percent Angus beef. To sleep on my Tri-Core pillow that provides great neck support, on a real mattress with box-springs, soft and supportive, easing back pain. So many little things and major ones, for which I am deeply appreciative, that before I took for granted. One may think, *I don't need to go to jail to appreciate what I have.* Is that certainly true? This is worthy of contemplation.

I felt good waking in this mindfulness, enveloped in love with a comforting hug from the Holy Spirit, gently reassuring me all is well. This is part of the plan; just relax, trust, *feel* healed. My distress and fears of failure, losing husband and family, were dispelled, finally, after I cried out to the Holy Spirit the previous night, asking, "Have You abandoned me? I need You!" I felt grateful and blessed to wake up in His embrace and healing.

# CHAPTER 37

# July 22nd

## LETTER TO MY HUSBAND

Dear sweetheart,

Day 67

Since I have two stamps left, let me use one to write my wish list, haha.

- shampoo
- soap
- stamps
- envelopes
- mouthwash
- pens
- TP
- summer sausage
- chicken breast
- cheese
- creamer
- meds, phone call $

Could you detach and mail me pages from coloring books?

Additional wish list: Amazon books on card game rules like Rummy 500 etc., and "The Book of Mysteries" by Jonathan Cahn. Luxury items: decaf coffee, chocolate, candy, desserts, honey buns, hot chocolate, cappuccino.

I love you and miss you. I want to come home to you! My friend didn't get to go home after all. Her ex prevented early release.

Tank drama continues. It's "Survivor," trustee style. Hanging in there as best as I can because I want to see you in October!

I love you very much! XOXO. Kiss the babies for me!

Me2

# CHAPTER 38
# Tuesday, July 23rd

## DAY 68: MEXICAN HUSBAND

Trustees moved in and out of the tank this week. Miriam left a few days ago. I miss my Christian-book-reading friend and her quiet support. I appreciated her commiseration, assessing that Tammy "is not a good, likable person." Since the toilet paper incident, my relationship with Tammy declines. Others are better able to "put up appearances" with her. Whenever she is absent, we sympathize with each other over her disagreeable personality.

Jan is stressed and quite down. Her attorney is unable to secure her early release. Her divorce judge favored the husband and refused to release her, calling her "a threat" to her ex's safety as well as to others. The judge believes the husband's tales of abuse, opposed to Jan's testimony, although it was backed in court with photographic evidence of her bodily bruises. We feel frustrated for her.

Lopez is set to leave Thursday. Her impending departure saddens me. She protects me. The girls have a roleplay game; at first, I was puzzled by their behavior, but after Lopez took me under her wing, mainly to protect me from Tammy's machinations, she began calling herself my "Mexican husband." Then

I realized the roleplay is all in good fun, not serious same-sex flirtations. I give Lopez my *panqueques* (pancakes) in exchange for her milk and "protection." We work mornings together. Her happiness is contagious. We giggle and chat through our work shift. One time Ms. Connor heard us giggling, and she unfairly yelled at us, threatening us both with discipline, "If I catch you doing that again, I will roll you immediately!"

Lauren joined us Monday as a new trustee. She has a quirky personality. She is exuberant, having way too much pent-up energy. She is charming, though. She makes me laugh. I like what she told me, "This is how I can deal positively with being locked up. I'm a fairy princess trapped in a dungeon waiting for my prince charming to slay the dragon and save me."

Tim gave me stressful news. In June, my mother-in-law lost one of her dogs, which I had rescued in 2008 from a Braum's hot parking lot. I gave this dog to my in-laws because my other dog, Maria, who I had since her birth in 2006, rejected Deedee (what I named the stray). Deedee succumbed to cancer just before my birthday. Now Tim's mother may have to put Lakota, another dog, down soon for her poor health. Additionally, his mom fell this past weekend, breaking her finger when her third and largest dog, George, a huge golden retriever, tripped her. My mother-in-law is having a difficult summer.

I experienced tension with my in-laws even before my downward spiral began with drinking and legal problems. Today, however, Tim astounded me, telling me that his sister feels bad about demanding I apologize to her. She is depositing a generous amount on my books. Flabbergasted, I wrote her an effusive "thank you" letter. He told me I would receive a commissary gift from both Mother and Sister. I am elated, very touched. At last, things with them are improving. They are finding forgiveness in their hearts for me, reaching out with unexpected support. God is answering fervent prayers I have petitioned Him with for years.

# CHAPTER 39

# Wednesday, July 24th

## DAY 69: ATW

This morning began normally, but at 11 a.m., just after Jan left for lunch service, a CO at the front desk suddenly called her over the intercom stating, "Get packed up ASAP, ATW!" Later, I learned that "ATW" means "all the way." We froze, looked at each other in shock, and Tammy yelled back, "She is working!"

"Where is she?" came the response.

"On the floor!"

"Oh, okay, I'll radio the CO then. Thanks."

Lopez, also on the floor working, bounced over to our window, pounded on it, and yelled that Jan was getting out. In a few minutes, our floor boss buzzed Jan back into the room. She was in disbelief, crying with joy as she packed up super fast, dumping her goods out on her bed, taking only that which was required to check out. Tammy quickly scooped up the commissary items and squirreled them away into her own basket, never to be seen again, naturally. Jan was at the door and gone in an instant, leaving us stunned in her wake but very happy for her.

If only I knew, I would have spent time with her that morning, talking, saying goodbyes... I was in a horrible mood, however, which puzzled me, following my glowing mood the previous day. Antisocially, I kept to my bunk after serving breakfast, writing, and reading.

After Jan left, I felt the loss of closure, but I will write to her soon.

# CHAPTER 40
# Thursday, July 25th

## DAY 70: LOPEZ IS FREE

This week continues to be stressful. Lopez was released at 1 p.m. For my sake, I am sad to see her leave, but for her sake, I am so happy. She is done now; her current charges dropped, just as she said God was going to do for her, freeing her legally to begin a new journey, hopefully staying out of trouble, which she asserted she would do.

New trustees include Kelli and Kinley, the first of whom is sweet and friendly, and the second seems a bit high maintenance, more standoffish. Kelli immediately introduced herself as she has spent today watching TV and chatting with me. She is very likable!

# CHAPTER 41

# Friday, July 26th

## DAY 71: MOURNING

Tammy has been crying, walking around, wringing her hands, moaning, "My girl, my girl… my girl is gone." She is taking Jan's departure hard. They worked nights together. Tammy leaned most heavily on Jan, constantly asking her to write letters to her lawyer and DA, pleading for lesser charges and bond release. Her letters were ignored. I suppose Jan felt relieved to get away from that pressure. Meanwhile, Tammy is cross and difficult for the rest of us, especially me. I am more vexed by her attitude every day.

Another new trustee arrived, who I shall call Francisca (meaning "free one"); her case troubles me. My judge gave her twenty-one days for driving with a suspended license two years ago. Since then, her driving privileges have been restored. She paid all fines, reinstating her driver's license. This unusually harsh sentence is senseless. She is anxious. She did not anticipate any jail time, which consequently has cost her her job. How unfair, detrimental, and needless. Francisca worries about paying rent, bills, and having her house plants watered.

# CHAPTER 42
# Saturday, July 27th

## DAY 72: FIGHTING

Kinley departed, and Earnestine arrived, a woman in her fifties, with long silver hair and a bigger build. She is "chill," as the younger women say, meaning laid-back and calm.

I had a big blowout fight with Tammy. During the toilet paper incident, I bit my tongue while, I am ashamed to say, making strangulation gestures at her back, being extremely upset with her TP denial for the rest of us. I started this new fight because I could not refrain verbally. I have always been uncomfortable when my temper rises. I would rather fly than fight, quickly departing a scene to avoid saying words later regretted, possibly having a lasting effect.

Tammy is terribly rude to the newbies. She is mourning Jan's departure and is tired of being locked up, as are we all. She is taking her frustration out on others as no one else is doing. Her rudeness is inexcusable. She has no reason to blame others for her misery.

When they were watching a program, she marched up to the TV and changed the channel, regardless. When they protested, she said, "I have been here the longest. I have seniority.

Therefore, I am 'tank boss.' So if you don't like it, bite me! I expect you to respect what I want as your senior."

At that, I just exploded, hotly retorting, "If you want respect, you have to show it, which you don't." I was uninterested in the program they were watching, but I defended them because they are all nice, sweet, respectful, and frankly, I "have been rooming with Tammy too long," as Kelli aptly surmised. Tammy's negativity, lies, and manipulations are wearing me down.

Tammy is confrontational and never backs down from a fight, so she "told me off" with expletives. I failed to take the higher road, shooting back at her.

The others are unimpressed with me beginning the fight. New to the situation, they are not used to Tammy's temperament. I realize now how I made myself look. I raised an alarm in them with consequential distancing. I feel ostracized, sensing their caution toward me. Honestly, I am ostracizing myself, blaming Tammy for it entirely.

# CHAPTER 43

# Sunday, July 28th

## DAY 73: RIGHTEOUS ANGER

Tension continues to build as Tammy treats the others with incredible rudeness. She is particularly mean to Lauren. Tammy keeps yelling at everyone else about respecting her, being quiet to let her sleep, turning the TV down when she needs sleep, but bumping up the volume considerably when she is watching it when others try sleeping. When the others asked her to turn the volume down, she rudely said, "No, deal with it!"

I retorted the same way, saying, "If you want respect, you have to show it!" As my anger increases, my temper worsens. I think of my anger as righteous since I stand up in defense of others, trying to get her to treat them better, to show *them* the courtesy they deserve because they *are* showing her respect, obeying her rules.

I think about how Jesus became angry at the mistreatment of others. His anger was righteous and therefore justified.[60] [61] God does not have a problem with righteous anger when it is in defense of the poor, oppressed, victimized, such as the case of Nehemiah standing up for the Israelites being abused.[62]

# JULY 28TH: LETTER TO MY HUSBAND

My dear love,

Day 73

I need to go home. I'm so tired of this drama. We have a new trustee. The one who gives others (mainly me) a hard time manipulates the others into being mean to the new one and to me since I stick up for her. The new one is young, bubbly, enthusiastic, and very sweet. But everyone else gangs up on her cruelly. I refuse to join in on the bullying, so I am on "the outs" too. I fear that's why the one I considered a friend didn't say goodbye or even look at me when she left: because the master manipulator had her mad at me too.

I failed God to make a positive difference, except to protect a couple of women who are otherwise picked on. They tried to roll this new, young one just because they dislike her, but she hasn't done anything wrong! She just needs guidance. I refused to sign, so naturally, I'm mud.

Please, God, send me home! I don't belong in this world!

I think the young one is strong and can defend herself. But I will always pick the side of the bullied, the underdog. I just don't understand why people have to be cruel. Why do they get off on it? If I'm irritable, I feel terrible about it.

Now they sit at the table whispering among themselves, passing notes, then tearing them up and flushing them, as if we can't figure out what they are doing.

At any rate, I've been guilty of it too, and I'm learning from God to stand up for the weaker or the picked on and to call out the meanness directly to the person's face and not to talk behind backs; God abhors gossip. The tongue truly is the devil's wicked weapon to wreak havoc, to hurt, to destroy, to tear apart...

Well, the manipulator did say to me yesterday, "This is jail, [bleep], it's supposed to be this way!"

I replied, "It doesn't have to be," and she said, "Yes, it does, so effin deal with it!"

Yep, time to go home. Enough punishment for me, new to jail and not belonging in this world. I would still minister to women in prison, though, given the opportunity. Please speak into existence me coming home ASAP.

Me2

# CHAPTER 44
# Monday, July 29th

## DAY 74: CHAMELEON

Tammy is exhibiting an amazing change in her attitude following our arguments over the weekend. She masterfully changes situations to her advantage, but the effect still pleases me, even if it means that I am excluded. She is suddenly considerate, generous, joking, sharing her food, making special treats. She stopped fighting over the TV or demanding unreasonable cooperation given its volume when others are sleeping.

Her objective is to alienate me from them. Her orchestration appears successful. They view me as the "bad guy." I may be wrong, but as long as they are happy and treated well, I am happier. I retreat to my bunk, keep to myself, and refrain from conversation.

I overheard them discussing how many of the COs are quitting because of understaffing, inmate overcrowding, and more lucrative positions elsewhere. I daydream of early release as I spiral downward emotionally.

# JULY 29TH: LETTER TO MY SISTER

Dear Lisa,

Day 74

I am incredibly grateful for prayers and Tim's intervention, slowly talking to my in-laws over time, changing their hearts. Now they express worry for me. They put money on my books! I appreciate it so much as I subsist on commissary and would have to do without except for the occasional hot dog or "schmicken" patty, tuna salad (otherwise known as "cat food") on the trays. Most of the time, they serve "brake pads" (some kind of bad-tasting soy/"schmeat" burger, very gross) and other mysterious forms of soy. The headache meds are great, too, since they cannot otherwise be obtained. I am well stocked and have $30 for phone calls. I'm good for at least two weeks. Do not worry.

With changes in "roomies" come new challenges. At first, it was a helpful distraction, and I thought I made a good impression on the new women, and we would all get along fine. All the original women, save for one, are gone. The remaining one has a very challenging personality, to say the least.

At first, I was taken in by her "sweet," sharing demeanor and her behavior, along with her stories of being a victim. Another woman who has since left was taken in at first also but became wiser to it, and a war started between the two, which lasted a month. I liked both women, but I was defending the "victimized" one and kept encouraging the other to be kind. The second woman in this equation left, leaving the "victim" here as the only original tankmate, as I mentioned. I was relieved and thought things would be easier, but such would not be the case. The dynamics in the room changed. With the new women, I watched the original one pick and chose who to befriend and who to bully.

At first, I let her manipulate me, unwittingly, about the others. Finally, I saw the light; then, seeing her be mean to the newbies was upsetting. I began standing up for the ones targeted for mocking and hostility, which put me on the original woman's bad side.

Now there is a "war" between us, and I hate it! I feel psychologically and verbally abused by her. When she does it to her targets, it seems they don't need me, however, to stick up for them. They handle it fine. One of the targets left thanking me for helping her; she hugged me and said several times she loved me. Another "ally" left four days ago, and she saw the BS as well, but it never got to her because she was strong, bright, and positive. She was also from the "hood." She was the nicest "bad" person I ever met (she described herself as "bad"). But she became protective of me.

With the new ladies now, in eighty-six hours, the manipulator has them all feeling sorry for her, and when she was mean to the youngest one, her newest target, I stood up for her, but it backfired, and with her feeding the fire, I suddenly see that I am being ostracized and whispered about. All I was trying to do was get the original woman to show some respect and consideration to others as she was demanding of them.

The oddest part of this is now that I am on the "outs," she is actually behaving the way I hoped that she would, except toward me. I am the new target, and this time I have no protection. I can't believe how easily she turned the tables to make me look mean. But one of the girls who left warned me that anyone who has been, or still is, addicted to dope becomes a master at manipulating others, essential for a tough life; many of them live on the streets. I'm just too soft, sensitive, and naive for this environment.

Right now, in this tank, considering all the hostility directed toward me currently, I'm considering once again whether it's worth it to remain a trustee. Tim would say definitely! He desperately needs me home. Once again, when I feel led to take action, another part of me resists and says, "Just let the chips fall where they may." Maybe they will all sign a form requesting I be rolled. It won't be for any good reason. Just that I'm moody because I'm collectively disliked at this point. Sometimes women who are rolled get to keep the two-for-one status if there's no major infraction, depending on circumstances.

I realize every tank has hostility and problems, the difference is I wouldn't have to work while feeling distressed about what's going on in here, and since I'm on edge emotionally, I end up crying in front of the guards, feeling embarrassed, as I make a fool of myself... but my adversary yesterday accused me of throwing pity parties for myself, crying all the time (I have cried daily for two weeks). I don't want sympathy. I don't want any attention when I'm crying/upset. I just want to hide until it's all gone and the environment returns to peace, harmony, respect, politeness, mutual consideration, and maturity. Meanwhile, my accuser constantly/daily throws self-pity parties and cries daily as well (almost all cry daily here!).

I ultimately conclude I will just follow the first rule: stay to myself and stay out of any arguments and drama.

I hope it's understandable that my light is almost out and my joy is gone. I'm begging God to help me with this. Christians all over the world in backward countries are being persecuted for their beliefs and tortured in prison daily, but retain their joy in the Lord and sing His praises anyway (good read, "The Insanity of God" by Nik Ripkin, true story...). How do they do it? And here I am crying over mean girls. How retarded is that? I need to get a grip! I'm not alone in battling depression. We all are. The original victim could be facing up to four years in TDCJ if none of her possession charges are dropped. She stays here fighting for a state sentence short enough that she can agree to (so I do feel bad for her, at least I know I'll get out soon).

This place is "getting" to me. I have paid my dues to society. I'm on my way to recovery. I feel much more confident about getting home and doing well, staying busy with God's work...

I'm sorry to write such a despondent letter. I hope my joy returns and spirits brighten again soon. Meanwhile, I'm hanging on the best I can, praying, meditating, writing, and sleeping. I can't currently focus on reading. My mind just wanders.

Thank you for your prayers and your positive affirmation daily: "Thank You, God, for releasing Shannon early" (or "soon" or "today").

Love ya always, Sis!

Shannypoo

PS: Approximately seventy-four days and counting, and still holding my mop, somehow.

# CHAPTER 45
# Tuesday, July 30th

## DAY 75: ROCK BOTTOM

Naturally, I suffer from bouts of self-doubt; at times, I give in to self-pity, being far from perfect. I spent the day writing about whether to roll back the general population.

"The Lord is my strength..."[63] After so much turmoil in the trustee tank, after two months and a week jailed, I arrived at my breaking point. Nothing happens without God's purpose and His permission since I put my life in His hands. I am meant to go through this trial. Today I feel part of the purpose of being here is to drive me to hate alcohol abuse, with a determination to avoid drinking completely. Being here is a sure test of faith.

My "protectors" are gone. All the ladies remaining form a gang of six who are against me because they fail to see that the tank master is deceiving them, just as I failed to see this at first, until my first protector, Ruth, left. I thought her departure was fortunate because the battle with Tammy departed with Ruth, but what actually happened is that I replaced Ruth. Tammy is powerful in her own right. She earns the sympathy from everyone around her. She turns people against each other. I dared to stand up for her targets. I had to call out injustice, but what a firestorm came back upon me. We are fighting dark principalities indeed.[64] I ultimately have victory in God, but I lost this battle because Jesus put too much love and compassion in my heart to disregard the unfair treatment of others.

I would only roll myself for work. I can suffer for Christ. I'm not fit to work because I cry, interfering with my ability to complete the job correctly as I fall apart emotionally. The COs do not need a basket case on the floor serving food trays.

The most distressing aspect of quitting trustee status is losing two-for-one, potentially putting me here well into next year instead of home by November. I will ask them to let me keep my two-for-one so I do not let my sweet husband down, who desperately wants me home by October's end. He begs me to persevere, but he doesn't understand the toll this is taking. I thought, naively, incarceration would be easier. I believed by shining God's light and love, I would be able to win women over for Him. Ironically, I feared physical violence, not psychological torment. When I first arrived, shining God's light seemed effective, but now I am worn out. My light is dim. My love is here, but buried under anguish, anxiety, hurt, rejection... none of that should matter. Having Jesus as my best friend and God as my employer, supply, strength, and protection should be all that counts.

If I roll, I must remember that all tanks have their problems. I could receive more abuse than I already endure. Perhaps even threats of physical violence, theft of commissary... but I would not be working, so it would be okay if I am a basket case. I would have a thinner mattress, hurting my bones more. The noise level would be horrific. Sleep could evade me, but I would endure, even as I suffer. I only spent five days total before becoming a trustee, but I remember feeling happier and more peaceful then.

What I might benefit from, God willing, are new alliances, friendships, and testimony. Renewed chances to learn of other's stories. I must trust God and give this time of incarceration to Him. If He truly wants me here until spring, so be it. If He allows me to go home sooner, it will be His perfect timing. I must be brave now for God, for Christ, and be committed to my spiritual faith and His work. How badly do I want out vs. how badly do I want a drink? I am imperfect, wrestling with my demons. This hell I currently feel is a compelling case for rock-solid commitment to sobriety.

I am changing for the worse relative to making a positive difference in other's lives, but it's constructive in my own healing. I thank God for forgiving me my uncontrollable angry outbursts. The last thing I ever want to do is hurt anyone. I detest being angry and hurtful. I fear each of these women think that of me. If so, they totally misunderstand. I only argued for the Gold Rule: treat others as you want to be treated.[65] Consideration is a two-way street. Be mutually respectful, considerate, and kind. What I endure now must be part of God's divine plan. Otherwise, God would have had it work out otherwise.

---

I have hit rock bottom, completely broken, with nothing left to give, around day seventy-five. As soon as the evening CO arrives, I'll submit my roll request. I may forsake a few items, like crackers, that I just received this morning, but I'll give anything I can spare that doesn't fit in my basket to the poorest person in the room, Ernestine, a kindly but sad woman my age, who looks ten years older due to hard street life, who hopes for outside help to post her bond, but none seems to be coming. She's the only one speaking to me today.

Completely broken. I opened my big mouth and got myself into this position by defending Lauren from bullying, but she turned around and stabbed me in the back at the first opportunity when she disliked hearing the word "no" only because I was trying to help Francisca, who needed an opportunity to work. Francisca begged me to be the one to "put my foot down" and "just tell Lauren" that she could not work the morning shift with me because Francisca has not yet worked (and Francisca does not want to work with Lauren, she insists she works with me). I wish Francisca had not put me in that position. Lauren cussed me out. I followed through with helping Francisca. Now it seems no one will speak to me other than Earnestine.

Anger got the best of me this week. My outburst began a few days ago. I couldn't stop my tongue. I am mortified with myself. I cried all morning. Now I look red-faced, blotchy, and puffy-eyed. A headache plagues me, as always when I cry. I feel pure misery. I have faith that I will keep my two-for-one time or get out early regardless. I pray for a miracle that anytime now, I'll hear the magic words: "Teichmann, pack up! You're going home!" A miracle happened for Jan last week, and it could happen for me too. I believe, I believe! Rock bottom brokenness means now Jesus can fill me up with His pure healing love, and I'm truly reborn in Him. I hate alcohol for the position it put me in so much now that I abhor the idea of ever touching it again. I only thirst for the living waters of Jesus Christ, my Lord and Savior. I've met many women, I've listened to their stories, and I have observed county jail life in Texas for seventy-five days. It's time to go home. Thank You, God. Amen.

# CHAPTER 46
# Wednesday, July 31st

## DAY 76: EMPTY VESSEL

I am a broken, empty vessel, ready for You to fill me with Your love, light, instruction. Mold and shape me, Lord, to Your liking. Keep me safe, protected, and warm as Your angel armies battle dark elements away. Thank You for sending me home. I pray in Jesus' sweet name, amen.

I am at peace, which comes with healed addiction and abhorrence of substance abuse.

Wine and spirits are not intrinsically evil, but their abuse and idolization of them. I made wine, tequila, and other spirits my idol, upon which I worshiped in an altar hidden in my closet. When I felt pain, I turned to my idol. When I wanted to celebrate, I turned to my idol. When I was angry, indignant, or even just arrogant, I turned to my idol. When God says, "Thou shalt have no other gods before me,"[66] He is referring to things of this world that pleasure us, that we, in turn, become enslaved to by overindulgence. Our loving, forgiving God realizes how easily this happens in a fallen world with Satan as our tempter, and He wishes to save, love, comfort, nurture and care for us. However, we must come to Him, seek Him willingly with an open, contrite heart.[67] The proud and arrogant do not want His forgiveness or help because they believe they have never done anything wrong. They believe they are perfect. So why would they seek forgiveness? Can God forgive those who won't receive it, who don't want it?[68]

*I come to You today, my Lord and Savior, seeking Your forgiveness, love, light, resurrection, living water, recognizing the error of my ways. I worshiped idols, false gods, of wine and spirits. Thank You so much, Lord, for forgiving me and loving me.* I just woke to this fact in the wee hours of the last morning of July in the year of our Lord 2019. Jesus set me free by breaking the alcohol-addiction chains that enslaved me. *God sets me free from jail to go home to my husband, fur babies, and family who need me, to finish healing, write this book, to begin the next new adventure of my life in service to Him, for His Glory, however He sees fit for me to work with Him to advance His kingdom. Amen.*[69]

---

The previous evening I planned to submit my request but chickened out in case it would cost me two-for-one time. I decided to ask first if I could roll and keep it. Later this day, I received the answer, simply stating I would, indeed, lose two-for-one if I roll myself.

I called my husband for a pep talk, allowing him to convince me to stay a trustee a little while longer because, as he put it, "things will inevitably improve." I decided my prayers and midnight meditations with epiphanies brought comfort, so God must be telling me to persevere. Ultimately, I surmounted this darkest night of my incarceration victorious in God. Through it, I gained a deeper understanding of the divinity of Jesus when he stated, "I am the resurrection and the life. The one who believes in me will live, even though they die…"[70] I felt like an empty vessel ready for the living waters of Jesus. We must empty ourselves first to be filled with His light, love, and life.[71] [72] [73]

I had an epiphany about fasting, a concept that dawned on me in my hour of need. I have been semi-fasting. Physical evidence shows in my diminishing size. I wore an extra-large uniform when first jailed. Now I wear mediums. When I studied the Bible directly and with guides, randomly, I opened pages that kept being about fasting, and I wondered why. Later I read in *Unbroken* the part about the men adrift at sea after their plane crashed. Hillenbrand describes how Zamperini had a vision after many days of starvation. He and Phil also had very lucid conversations.[74]

Although I am not fully fasting and I am nowhere near starvation, I suddenly understand that fasting leads to clarity of the mind. Hence, this is the reason Jesus told His disciples, "… this kind goeth not out but by prayer and fasting,"[75] answering His disciples' question why they failed to exorcise the multiple-demon possessed boy and had to call Jesus to get the job done. Hence, my mind is clearer about my deeper understanding of Jesus as the living waters, His divinity, why He is the resurrection, the life, and how this relates to becoming an empty vessel in order to be filled by the Holy Spirit.

## JULY 31ST: LETTER TO MY HUSBAND

My dearest husband,

Day 76

Yesterday I broke, becoming the empty vessel God was waiting for. I tipped over and completely emptied. I sobbed all day until no more tears were left, completely spent. The scripture came to me about being completely emptied so I could be filled up, rebuilt exactly as God needs me in order to serve Him in whatever kind of ministry He has in store.

Being broken means truly being set free from the bondage of addiction and fear of its return. Alcohol isn't intrinsically evil. Worshiping it as a false idol through Satan-induced slavery via addiction is evil. I am not intrinsically evil, but weak in my humanness, born into a fallen world with a fleshly body given to a sinful nature, but redeemed in the rebirth of Jesus Christ within, fed by His living water, thirsting only for that and nothing of this world beyond what God created to give us pleasure in a judicial, prudent, limited use.

The fear is gone. I'm certain this hell I'm in is not worth it. I've rested and healed enough to know at the deepest level I'm free. Now I crave freedom to return home to you, your warmth, love, protection, and our sweet fur babies. Gone completely is fear of desire for alcohol, replaced by a readiness to embrace an exciting and prosperous future per God's will.

Thank You, God, for freeing me in more ways than one. From addiction, fear of it, and from jail. In Jesus' sweet, precious name, I pray, amen.

I love you, miss you terribly, and will be home in your arms again soon.

Me2

# CHAPTER 47
# Thursday, August 1st

## DAY 77: ANGEL

I met a woman recently at rec who is very sweet and kind to me. She's an angel watching over me, so I call her "Angel." She approached me, saying that she heard about Tammy's behavior toward me and the others. Apparently, Tammy's reputation is spreading to other tanks. The toilet paper incident has become well known. My reputation also is circulating, but according to Angel, mine is good, thankfully. I am gratified to hear women in other tanks speak well of me. Angel told me she applied to be a trustee and hoped to be approved, saying if she is, she wants to watch out for me and protect me from Tammy. She said that many women want to be a trustee but refrain from applying because of Tammy.

Lo and behold, today, they approved Angel's request, and I am delighted she joined us. I am so happy to have a new ally. Angel speaks her mind fearlessly. She announced to the tank, "As long as I am here, no one is messing with Shannon. She is too sweet for that." Then she hugged me.

Angel reminds me of Bahati only in that she has fashioned a T-shirt as a turban around her head. She is much younger than Bahati, though, tall and beautiful with high cheekbones and full lips, looking something like a tribal princess. She emanates love and kindness, counting the most, of course.

## AUGUST 1ST: LETTER TO MY HUSBAND

My dear sweet Tim,

Day 77

I received your sister's amazing gift today, and I wrote and posted a thank you letter to her already. I was blown away and very appreciative. I might not need anything else except money for phone calls to you, toilet paper, and meds until I get out!

I'm enclosing an updated price list just so you can see the ridiculous jump in the cost of commissary items.

I began drawing portraits of the girls at their request! They also ask me to draw them fairies, angels, devils, etc. They love the drawings!

Could you order me two coloring books? The sophisticated kind? Intricate patterns, animals, whatever... The designs are probably the best kind. Thanks.

I sent a letter to my judge too.

Love you! XOXO,

Me2

# CHAPTER 48

# Saturday, August 3rd

## DAY 79: DEVIOUS

I am honestly angry with Tammy. She is amazingly cruel sometimes. I guess Angel's declaration that she would not allow anyone to "mess with" me did not go over too well with her. Friday is laundry day. Tammy, being here the longest, has the choicest work assignments and gets out of the tank the most. She helps the commissary lady distribute orders. She helps the evening COs pass out indigent supplies. She helps the laundry CO collect dirty laundry every Friday. Each CO she assists holds her in high regard because she is smart, fast, works hard, and learns new tasks quickly. I will give Tammy that. Tammy also lies to them, turning on her tears, telling them we bully her, portraying herself as a victim in all circumstances, including her charges, in which she claims innocence. Tammy is that good. The COs believe her.

Tammy noticed Angel's "turban," in that it is made from a jail-issued T-shirt. Destruction of state property, in this case, obviously, jail property, is prohibited and up for discipline. Tammy, therefore, found the ammo she needed to "solve" this situation with Angel, to remove someone who would protect me. She snitched to the laundry CO that Angel destroyed a jail-issued

T-shirt in the process of fashioning her headdress. Angel defended herself, claiming the T-shirt belonged to someone else who left it behind, and it was eventually given to Angel for the purpose of making the head covering, but the laundry CO was incensed and immediately rolled her. I am disgusted by the situation.

However, I am strangely peaceful about it because Angel is now safe from Tammy's machinations. I think Angel is not facing further discipline over the cut-up T-shirt beyond being rolled. Tammy's "reporting" of Angel sheds a new light on Renee and Raven: Tammy reported them to the same laundry CO, who was the one to roll them. Tammy must have noticed how well I was getting along with them. Tammy told me she had them rolled to protect me. I now realize that her motives were probably different from what she claimed.

## AUGUST 3RD:
## LETTER TO MY HUSBAND

My dearest, sweetest, most loving husband,

Day 79

I'm out of money for phone calls. I had to buy extra pads from the floor boss and was charged for shaving razors; although trustees are supposed to get these free as a "perk" for working, we are charged for them anyway, seventy cents each; they only give us one hour to use them. Depending on how many times you want me to call you, I need funds. Here's a list of items I order regularly. Most are not on the public website. Keep in mind there's a new price increase:

- 0571, Chlorophen x 10, $5.50
- 0583, Ibuprofen x 4, $1.50
- 0500, Mouthwash x 1, $1.60
- 0770, Toilet paper x 4, $4.60
- 2011, Decaf coffee, $5.25
- 2017, Maxwell House Coffee, $6.15
- 6421, Ranch dressing x 2, $2.00
- 2087, Creamer x 5, $5.10
- 3585, Summer sausage x 1, $3.30
- 6520, Oatmeal x 3, $2.25
- 6422, Cheddar cheese bar x 1, $2.50
- 6459, Mozzarella cheese bar x 1, $2.50
- 6540, Cereal bar, $.95
- 6195, Chicken, $4.85

Luxuries I wish I could order:

- 2041, Cappuccino, $3.45
- 2071, Cocoa, $3.40
- 4146, Atomic Fireballs, $2.00
- 4000, M&Ms, $1.65
- 6606, Peanuts, $1.05
- 6217, Tropical Mix, $1.90

I'm always grateful for everything. I'm certain after receiving the huge gift package from your family I won't need any more. The candy, though, is useful for trading and cheering the girls up.

All of this is not a matter of life or death. I feel bad for those who have no one on the outside to hook them up. Makes me self-conscious. Everyone watches out for number one. Hard as a Christian, Jesus instructs us not to deprive others of their needs. If one doesn't have enough to share equitably, it makes sense not to, right? Sometimes we each do share by contributing something in the creation of a snack shared with all.

Love you always,

Me2

## AUGUST 3RD: LETTER TO MY SISTER

Dear Lisa,

Day 79

We just spoke yesterday by phone, but I'm bored. According to Tim's calculations, the week of August 19th qualifies me for possible early release, having served two-thirds of my sentence if they count two-for-one. I don't know if the jail will be overcrowded again or if they would consider me. I wrote a letter to the judge too, asking for consideration, it's within his power to do that, but he is stricter than other judges; however, you never know. Anyway, I'm praying and writing positive affirmations every day with August 28th as a target date, and it will work if it's in God's plan.

I'm happier in my tank since I swallowed my pride and apologized to everyone, bringing mutual sentiments; everyone settled down. They seem happy again, saying, "It's okay, I was wrong too." Now I just mind my own business, stay out of tiffs, let others defend themselves. They don't want my help; it works out and reverts to normal. The whole overly dramatic episode and day of crying led to a "rock bottom" moment I needed, emptying me out. I felt completely broken. Then I remembered scriptures about that, and when it happens, God can rebuild us and fill us with His "living waters," i.e., Spirit, shaping and molding us into who He wants us to be to fulfill our divine purpose.

It was a breakthrough because I felt suddenly freed from fear of future addiction and inability to overcome the desire to drink... to be clear-minded and focused on the work God has in store for me. When God says we cannot serve two masters, He means to focus on and complete the work of our divine purpose while not also being consumed by earthly desires like excessive drink, drug use, sex addiction, gluttony—anything that leads to unhealthy, unbalanced lifestyle, fogging the mind.

The entire experience, as miserable as it was, strengthened me through adversity, deepened my understanding of walking with God. Learning the stories of these women has given me some beautiful moments when I was able to encourage and up-lift spirits with God's love, sharing tears and renewed hope with them as they are all broken too. We are talking about cases that are much more severe than anything I experienced personally... These women are beautiful and loving in their brokenness, far from monsters a cold society judges. Their addictions evolved out of extremely broken homes, some with crack parents who molested and neglected them, etc. At young ages, they ended up living on the streets or in one motel room after another, some-times having sex for the next high, and many, if not most times, losing children they had because of their life of drugs and crime on the street.

I realize you have personal knowledge of cases like these from your experience adopting children. I love these women, God loves them, and each one is redeemable and precious to Him, and if they let Him, He can heal them and use them for

His purposes while bringing them blessings and prosperous lives. That is what He is doing with me.

For the first time in my life, I feel like a worthwhile person. All my life, I felt worthless and undeserving of anything good. I don't know why I was so hard on myself and had such a low self-esteem. Now I have victory in Jesus, God, and the Holy Spirit. I feel strong, vibrant, smart, accomplished because I can do all things in Christ who strengthens me. I can show His love to others, and that is such a joyful, love-filled moment.

Well, I'm tired, my hand hurts, and so I will close.

Love ya!

Shannypoo

PS: Congrats again on the new home and move! Yay! I can't wait to see it in person someday.

# CHAPTER 49

# Sunday, August 4th

## DAY 80: BOSSY TRAINER

The longer I go through God's assignment, the more He challenges me. He is teaching me patience and the type of love Paul describes in his epistles, such as the famous one, 1 Corinthians 13:4-7, "Love is patient, love is kind...."[76]

For example, this morning, I was working with Lauren, who I cannot train because she "knows what she is doing," as she puts it. She knows all things, needs not be taught anything. She calls me "bossy." At first, I had a difficult time with this, which served as one of the catalysts prompting my emotional breakdown. She was rude to me again this morning. She actually commands *me* on what to do. She treats me disrespectfully. Then I think, *She knows not what she does. Perhaps her parents did not teach her, and she had a difficult upbringing like many women here, myself included.* As Jesus said on the cross, "Father, forgive them, for they know not what they do."[77] So I must forgive her, even if she does not seek it, because she only sees that she does "no wrong." I must be patient and kind, in Christ's image, abiding in Him. *Father, I pray, help me when I am angered, irritated, or hurt by the rudeness of others. Please help me to quell negative emotions quickly, to remember not to take anything personally, and just to bless, love, and pray for them instead.*

So I told myself to step back and let her shine as she so desires. Be the support person in the background. This is important to her but not to me. I realize that being renewed and reborn in Christ, I am no longer invested in trivial matters. What of it if she makes mistakes? If she isn't open to correction, I cannot help her anyway. The CO either chooses to step in or not. Perhaps the floor boss, in this case, Ms. Hughes, sees me as failing in my role as "trainer" but more than likely perceives the situation as it is. We are only serving food trays. If accidents happen, they happen.

An accident happened with my last morning coworker Lopez. Training her was challenging as well. She was always friendly and upbeat, though. She went ahead of me to push the big, heavy kitchen cart of fresh, hot food trays through a doorway partitioning our hallway from male and female sections. I yelled, "Stop! Wait!" but she didn't hear me and the cart hit the side of the doorway, spilling four trays, spreading food all over the floor. Mrs. Hughes was so mad she cussed at us. We cleaned the mess up while she ordered replacement trays. My coworker's contriteness and apology calmed her down. Lopez learned from this mistake. However, it took the accident to teach her because she ignored my instructions. She ignored other instructions, making the process of tray distribution cumbersome. If I suggested a change, her stock response was, "It doesn't matter." She did not anger me, though, because she was so likable, charming, and bright. She made it easy to forgive her and overlook what bothered me, shrug it off and move on.

Lauren makes it more challenging for me to get over as she is bossy and disrespectful. Mornings are especially difficult because she wakes up grumpy, often yelling or speaking loudly and cussing. I pray continuously for God's help in making me patient and kind, to shine His love even when I feel put out. Regardless of these challenges, Lauren and I reach common ground sometimes as we like the same type of TV programming, which we can enjoy when Tammy is out working or asleep.

I also need to keep in mind that Lauren's allergies are wreaking havoc on her. She blames the mold, which not only grows on the inside wall from rain leaks but in the shower stall as well. Physically she feels miserable. She submitted a request for the mold to be cleaned, concerned it may be "black mold." The only answer received was that "it would be looked at," with the added question, "Does this resolve the complaint? If so, sign and return." So she signed, and naturally, no one ever came to assess the mold.

When Tim and I spoke last night, he shared his woes, telling me how lonely he is, how home is not home without me, how he longs for my return. He said he has a new appreciation of how much work the dogs take to let in and out, walk, feed, water, and comfort during storms and UPS visits. I am convinced the separation strengthens our marriage and is beneficial in fueling his ambition to get his rock band off the ground, gig-ready by summer's end. This is a trial for us both and will help him achieve greater success. He is learning the importance of standing up for and protecting his wife from harsh criticism. I am learning I need to change in life to successfully stay with Tim without drinking. Alcohol was my coping mechanism. Challenging relations served as my triggers (not causes). If people and circumstances cannot change, then the last resort is to change places (change places, people, and things, as the AA saying goes). Leaving my husband would be heart-shattering and is not an option. Despite the often negative episodes with which we have to cope, our marriage is strong and happy. We are deeply in love. We agree our love continues to grow, deepen, and strengthen. We recognize how blessed we are.

# CHAPTER 50
# Wednesday, August 7th

## DAY 83: REFLECTIONS

Tammy is still stirring up trouble, causing arguments, attacking me, others, keeping things riled up. She is still lying about all of us to the COs, but I think they know us better than to believe we are really bullying her. Satan will attack from any avenue available.[78] Those who disbelieve he exists, as used to be the case with me, are unaware of the negativity for which they open themselves. I pray vigilantly for protection not only of my own person but for the entire tank, "I claim this space in the name of Jesus Christ, our Lord and Savior. This tank is filled with light and love—so much so that all dark entities are chased away. God's angel armies protect us from the dark forces.[79] [80] I wear God's armor, as described by Paul in Ephesians, chapter 6."[81] I also pray, "Please bind here what is bound in heaven," per Matthew 18:18.

Once upon a time, I was completely unaware evil truly exists. My parents taught me that there is no devil with evil minions. I mimicked them, making fun of people who believed in the dark principalities, which pains me now. I failed to realize the danger I was in, left unprotected, wide open to attack, in my naivety, much to Satan's delight. He needs the world to disbelieve he exists so he can successfully turn humans away from God and their divine purpose, for which God created them.

---

One of the librarians was a believer and prayer warrior at the academic library where I worked. She calls herself an "intercessor,"[82] praying on behalf of others being attacked by Satan, such as the time I cried following an argument with a coworker. She said, "The devil is attacking you! I'll pray for you! I'm an intercessor!" I had no idea what she meant. I "read" the Bible cover to cover twice in my life, taking me over a year (actually skimming much). I failed to understand a majority of it, lacking in-depth study guides, reliable commentary, and insight from the Holy Spirit. God's Word mystified me; it seemed enigmatic, difficult to comprehend. Sadly, I had "bashed" the Bible prior to becoming a Christian, along with other non-believers. I ridiculed "fundamentalist" Christians similarly to how our secular culture does currently. Disbelievers find true followers of Christ to be "crazy" lunatics.

Disbelieving librarians I worked with joined me in gossip about the intercessor-librarian. We avoided her as much as possible. Actually, other Christian coworkers found her annoying, proud, dictatorial, a "know-it-all" with an air of superiority, who perceived her own perfection. At least she came across that way. We are all human beings, flawed, yes, even true followers of Christ. Only Christ, God incarnate, was/is truly perfect. Much of what the intercessor-librarian said seemed senseless. When I felt unwell, she said, "You are healed by his stripes[83] and cleansed by His blood,[84] so stand on the scriptures, and you will be healed." In the third part of this statement, she may have been referring to scriptures about standing firm, such as in 2 Thessalonians 2:15

(NIV): "So then, brothers and sisters, stand firm and hold fast to the teachings we passed on to you, whether by word of mouth or by letter."

I thought, *What? How? Huh?* How would any of this make sense to one without studying the Bible in-depth and seeking God for His wisdom to gain a deeper understanding of His Word from the Holy Spirit? However, she planted seeds that later bloomed after I came to Christ and subsequently gained the opportunity for deep Bible study at church, especially after I began teaching Sunday school. Years later, I experienced many "aha!" moments, thinking, *So that is what she meant!*

One time I showed her a new car I bought and how it included Sirius XM, with many channels from which to choose. She said, "I only listen to gospel. Anything else secular has no interest to me. The same for television."

I was astonished. I asked, "You mean you don't enjoy *anything* that's not Christian programming?"

"Yes, that is what I'm saying," she responded.

Only years later, after studying Lamentations in Sunday school, did I begin to comprehend her point. Eventually, secular entertainment and much of the secular world began to lose much of its appeal to me as well.

If I worked at that college now, I would be an outcast for how I changed. The non-Christian librarians, staff, faculty, and students would have avoided me like the plague. Very few truly followed Christ and would have related to me. Before I left the college, I began transforming, becoming sympathetic to my weird Christian coworker. I watched *The Bible* on the History Channel in 2013[85], not expecting at the time for it to touch me the way that it did. In my humble opinion, that production was anointed by God. The show was excellently cast, and the actor portraying Christ skillfully depicted His deep love and compassion. All the actors were convincing. The Old Testament stories were performed superbly, but the New Testament episodes touched me deeply, planting magical seeds that later bloomed.

Years later, as I studied the Bible for the first time, little nuggets of wisdom previously planted sprang to life, blooming into bigger epiphanies. Eventually, I became uncomfortable at the academic library. I believed in Christ as God incarnate for the first time, and the teasing, gossiping, and avoidance of the intercessor-librarian began to prick my conscience. Eventually, I could no longer gossip. I kept my silence, though, as a seedling sprouting into a true Christian for fear of ridicule and ostracism. Additionally, I tread carefully due to professional rules of leaving religion and politics at home (although in academia, any religion other than Christianity, as well as atheism, seems welcome discourse, sometimes celebrated). The Christian librarian seemed unaware of her own ostracism. She appeared blind to herself as to the effect she had on others. When others criticized her, she was stoic. She had strength in rising above hostilities and people's coldness.

Unlike her, I am hyper-aware and too sensitive. I was sadly too cowardly to speak up, stand up, and say who I really was in that environment. All I could do was shine as much of God's light and love as possible, avoiding being judgmental. I performed small acts of kindness whenever possible. Verbally I did not credit the source except toward the end of my time there when it became evident I was leaving.

I could see the end approaching at the college a year after my new boss was hired. The previous boss, who retired, was kindly and tolerant of diverse views, even when he disagreed. The new boss had a low level of tolerance. Not long after she realized I was opposite her politically, her attitude toward me changed dramatically, from friendly to almost hostile. This new work situation prompted me to ask God for His direction. I told my husband, "I am at a crossroads. I do not know what exactly is coming, but big changes lay ahead."

---

In the autumn of 2016, my in-laws began attending church services. My husband and I waved at them as they drove by on Sunday mornings. When I noticed their new routine, I was unaware of its purpose. One Sunday morning, I asked Tim, "Where are they off to?"

"Oh, Doug's gotten on this religious kick. They are exploring churches to find the one they like." We both snickered.

"You won't see me going to church," I laughed. "Churches make me feel like I'm suffocating." Truthfully, I longed to find a church home, but churches I had visited felt oppressive in some inexplicable way; people seemed unwelcoming.

"I won't go to church because of their hypocrisy and politics. God is not in a church building. He's right here, in my heart," Tim answered, pointing at his chest.

"Here, here," I cheered, raising my coffee mug to him.

Soon Doug began inviting me to church. He found one he liked, attending every Sunday and Wednesday night Bible study, along with his wife (Tim's mother). At times, Doug urged her to call me and extend the invitation. "Well, okay," I reluctantly agreed. Sunday morning, without fail, I called her to cancel with typical excuses, "I'm too tired," or, "I don't feel well." At times I cited the weather. When I crossed Doug's path while he drove the Gator around the property, he stopped and warmly invited me again, with joyful expectation. I noticed him change; he seemed more positive, upbeat, happier. He began praying over meals when we joined them for Thanksgiving and Christmas celebrations. He never gave up asking, urging me to join them at church. I kept resisting. "Maybe next weekend…"

Finally, after Christmas and New Year, Doug asked me once more to join them. I realized he would persist until I accepted. I thought, *I'll go, and afterward, I'll explain, "Well, that wasn't my 'cup of tea,' but thank you for inviting me anyway."* That would end the matter. God had other plans.

When I walked through the doors of this small country church, I anticipated cold or incurious looks, meaningless handshakes, and empty words of welcome, lacking true warmth, my typical experience in the past. Granted, they usually weren't small country churches but urban denominations like Methodist, Lutheran, Catholic, and even Unitarian. I had no idea what I was headed into. Opposite of my expectations, the congregation greeted me with boundless love and warmth, evident in their handshakes, hugs, eyes, and smiles.

Suddenly, joy and enthusiasm seized me. I cannot adequately describe what happened physically, but I felt like my heart was suddenly bursting with love, and I wanted to dance for joy. After announcements, when the praise and worship music began, I was dancing, waving my arms, tapping my feet, and a big smile split my face. I glanced over at my in-laws, with Doug smiling and Mom standing still beside me. I thought, *They probably think I'm crazy, but that's all right.*

My response astonished me. The only church I attended in my life where I did not feel suffocated was Unity Church of Christianity, where my parents attended. When I visited traditional Christian churches, I felt negative, immediately desiring to flee. I mentally blocked any chance I might enjoy service and receive a constructive message from the pastor.

Raised in a New Age, metaphysical philosophy, taught that the devil and evil do not exist, makes me struggle with the concept of eternal damnation. My mother said hell is only a state of mind after crossing over and the soul becomes trapped by guilt, disbelief in an afterlife, denial of the body's physical death, or trapped by the body's physical and mental addictions. Perhaps hell is something like this, but in a metaphysical philosophy typical of a 1970s home with hippy-like parents, eternal damnation and condemnation were a fiction. As Lee Strobel questioned in *The Case for Christ*, how could a loving God condemn his creations to an eternity without Him, especially with everlasting torture?[86] (Strobel discusses D. A. Carson's answer to these questions on pages 222 and 223.) Hence, I admit I still struggle with accepting eternal damnation. My parents taught reincarnation instead, adapted from eastern philosophies, where souls return to earth again and again in a cycle of education and purification to the point that the soul is advanced enough to "become one with God," or "achieve nirvana." My biased mindset against traditional Christian teachings of everlasting hell and damnation, coupled with prejudice that their congregations were judgmental, condemning, and "holier than thou," undoubtedly contributed to my feelings of suffocation, born out of misunderstanding, trepidation, and fear. I imagine this delightfully amused Satan.

However, the Holy Spirit intensely fills this small country church, well off the beaten path, with a dwindling, aged congregation. I left forever changed, newly in love. I could only credit the Holy Spirit for this change: newfound joy, overflowing love from my heart, fascination in every word from the pastor's sermons. I am convinced God saved me. He reached down and plucked me out of the darkness, retrofitted me for His purposes and plans. He chose me, called me. I am incredibly grateful and undeserving, but thankful for, as I was in a dark place.

---

Sometimes I drank too much. I had at times over the years, but it eventually became more consistent. Mostly, I consumed alcohol on the weekends. I knew my drinking was potentially problematic, yet I had no intention of quitting permanently. Yet, at times I felt a madness I wanted to stop. I was conflicted. Deep down, I knew wine was holding me back from spiritual growth, a relationship with God, and a healthier, stronger marriage. The only two things my husband and I fought about were money and my drinking. Together, both of our incomes combined barely covered our bills, gas, and groceries, with nothing left over. What I spent on wine didn't help.

I grew tired of weekend hangovers, headaches, and faded memories. I was obese. My doctor warned me that my extremely high cholesterol and obesity would kill me via heart attack. Life was stressful. Working hard to make ends meet, my husband and I lacked time and money for vacations, real "R and R." We just "kept on keeping on," as often is the case for the working poor. My husband is a locksmith, and paid jobs, as well as his paychecks, fluctuate. My husband and I always treated one another with love, kindness, and respect. We immensely enjoy our "fur babies." Ultimately, we make the best of things. I regretted disappointing him with my drinking and quit multiple times, managing a few months to a year at a time. I attended AA meetings sporadically.

In my youth, I had occasional bouts of drinking from eighteen to thirty-two years of age. I despised excess drinking, eschewing alcohol from months to years. I grew up in an alcoholic home from age eleven when my mother married my stepfather, a heavy drinker. I had an alcoholic spouse from 2001 to 2006. I quit drinking entirely during the five years we spent together. I loathed what I saw alcohol do to him as I had my stepfather. I loved him so much I gave him five years, hoping he would heal, find peace and sobriety. Doing so with God's help was out of the question because he was a devout atheist. I believed in God but lacked a close relationship with Him.

When that relationship ended in December 2006, I forced him to depart completely from my life, and I thought, *Now I can enjoy an occasional glass of wine.* After this, my drinking began, slowly escalating over a decade. By 2017, I was ready to find peace in sobriety. I had spent years by this point periodically in an alcoholic fog. I wanted health. I desired life. I was, certainly, dead in my sin.[87]

When the Holy Spirit rescued me that January Sunday morning, I was ripe for reception beyond my own comprehension. I knew, without doubt, I was forever changed. I was so joyful I soon began to testify. This should have ended my drinking. I was mostly sober during the first year of salvation. Events on the horizon, however, served to trigger it again, and my struggle renewed with a long and arduous battle.

———

After the first Sunday at my new church home, I was excited to ride along with Doug and Mom to Wednesday night Bible study. I was just as thrilled Wednesday evening with the Holy Spirit so present, filling the fellowship hall with love and joy. I could not "get enough." We ate dinner first, and then the pastor gave his lesson. We rode home feeling happily content. During the twenty-minute drive home, I asked Doug why he chose to attend church "at this time," referring to the past year of 2016, after many years. "It was just time," he simply answered, smiling in the rearview mirror.

Ten minutes after they dropped me off, my husband's phone rang. He was in the shower. I normally wouldn't look at his phone, but the ring tone alerted me that his mother was calling. I thought, *That's odd, they just got home.* Doug and Mom lived next door. They owned both homes on a rural property. We rented the smaller of the two from them. I could walk next door in less than a minute. My inner alarm sounded. I answered his phone. As soon as I said, "Hello," Mom's panicked voice yelled, "It's Doug! Something's wrong! Come quick!"

"I'll be right there. Tim's in the shower. I'll tell him to hurry and come ASAP."

"Hurry, please!" she cried. I should have told her to call 911 in the meantime. A few months before, she called Tim in a similar panic. We hurried over to find Doug recovering from a sudden drop in blood sugar. He went to the hospital but was not on the brink of death. I find it easy to look back and think, "I should have done… I should have known…"

When I arrived, she urged, "Hurry! He's in his office! I don't know what to do!" She was crying, fully panicked. When I rounded his desk and saw him lying on the floor, I looked right into his eyes and gasped, "Oh Doug!" as I witnessed the last light twinkle out and his lids close. "Call 911!" I exclaimed. She was in no mental state to take decisive action, in such shock. I had my iPhone, so I pulled it out of my pocket, dialed 911, and hit the speaker button. The operator answered immediately. I set the phone on Doug's chair, from which he had slumped off to the floor. I quickly described the situation, and the operator dispatched emergency response, then proceeded to walk us through CPR. We took turns. I kept thinking, *He's already gone!* At times I cried out, "Come back, Doug!" I felt so helpless, ignorant, and uneducated as to what to do in an emergency.

Tim arrived and helped us stretch Doug out because he fell at an odd angle. His head was propped up on a box in his tiny office. I asked Tim to take over, but he said, "No, you're doing fine. I have to go out and guide the fire department in." We lived down a narrow gravel road. Their driveway curves as well. *Thanks a lot, Tim!* I thought in desperation. CPR was not reviving Doug, and I was unsurprised. I knew in my gut he was gone. I felt like a total failure. However, one cannot stop administering CPR just because it may not work. One can never assume anything in this situation. Any moment a miracle could happen. I thought, *Jesus, You could send him back!*

So remote is our location, first responders only arrived after twenty minutes, the most stressful and heartbreaking of my life. They took over, carrying him out on a stretcher. The operator valiantly walked us through, step by step, for over twenty minutes. We thanked her profusely and hung up, and I drove Mom to the hospital, following the ambulance. Shock and numbness set in. I found it incredible that just an hour before, they dropped me off after a lovely evening at church.

Doug officially passed away the following Monday, although I knew, in reality, he passed the first moment I saw him lying on the floor. However, that call was never mine to make. Waiting in a private room for family members having loved ones in ER, Mom discussed with her daughter, who arrived shortly after us from her own residence, Doug's status, clearly belying lack of acceptance he was gone. Who was I to chip in and say, "Let him go, Mom." You never know about that miracle. The ER physician came in and was honestly straightforward, although he spoke gently, patiently, compassionately. Doug lacked oxygen to his brain for forty minutes. Paramedics only revived Doug's heartbeat upon arrival at ER. The ER doctor said, quite frankly, that Doug was gone. He recommended removing life support. Even if his body continued to live, he would be brain dead. Mom alone had to decide. We could understand her inability to let go and her desire to give him every chance for a miraculous recovery. Tim and I agreed that we would choose to do that for each other as well.

---

Subsequent to Doug's passing, I drank sporadically from January through March. I quit drinking after my brother recommended I investigate getting the sleeve surgery. I discovered by the beginning of May that my health insurance covered it fully. I began preparing my body for surgery by replacing two meals a day with shakes and light eating. I lost twenty-five pounds prior to surgery, scheduled in July.

Work stressed me as rapport with my boss rapidly deteriorated. By May, she made it clear I was unwelcome, finding the slightest reasons to chastise me. She explicitly told me that she did not want to hear my opinion on anything, instructing me not to speak at all except to answer her direct questions. I was to "keep my mouth shut," and if I upset her, she would "write me up." I felt distraught. I never experienced this degree of animosity before on any job. I was verbally guided regarding job improvement but never formally rebuked to this extent or "written up."

However, God answered my prayers. After Doug passed, I prayed for my husband to get a new job quickly since Doug owned the locksmith company that employed him. Within a few weeks, Tim's locksmith friend, who ran his own company, hired him. I prayed for my sister-in-law to find new employment, as Doug also employed her. She found a good job by the end of 2017. Aramark food services, my son's employer, fired him in January that year. Subsequently, his car broke down beyond repair in April. He was stuck at home, no longer in college, so I drove him to the local US Navy recruiter. He excelled at their testing, and once he contemplated the excellent career opportunities they offered him, given his high marks, he enlisted and was off to boot camp by June.

After praying for my own employment, a law librarian position came open to which I applied in June. I could have the sleeve surgery before leaving the college if the new employer agreed to wait until August. After I interviewed for the position, they initially offered the job to someone else, who decided against it after working one day. Then they offered it to me. I contemplated it for a few days and felt God guide me to accept it. After eleven years at the college, I was scared to take a chance, but I knew things would not go well otherwise. I took a leap of faith and accepted the position when my new employer agreed to wait until mid-August for my start date, allowing me to have surgery, take one week off for recuperation and complete my notice at the college.

Normally, two to three months is recommended to recuperate from bariatric surgery, but I lacked the luxury of time, which was stressful. I had to push myself hard to wrap things up, move all my personal effects out of my old office, take a quick three-day road trip to see my son graduate from boot camp north of Chicago, and then go straight to my new job. Additionally, my first assignment was to pack up the existing library, weed ninety percent of the print collection, and move it into a much smaller space. So immediately after beginning the new job, I was involved in quite a bit of physical labor.

By the grace of God, I managed it, pleasing my new employers, setting up a lovely, small library from which to serve the public. God helped me greatly to quickly learn my new responsibilities, so I could effectively serve the community; it was a crash course! I lacked prior legal experience. My courthouse colleagues and the public liked me. I dropped weight fast, down a size each month. Despite the short recuperation time, I had energy.

I felt so good! I had zero desire to drink. Things were off to a great start. I strongly felt the job change was God's plan to move me in new directions where I would be of greater help to people truly in need. Most patrons were poor, desperately needing help, unable to afford legal representation. Legally, how I could help them was limited, but I could guide them to locations of statutes and forms to search, as is the role of any librarian, regardless of subject. I was so happy at work the first few months.

However, I did not see challenges on the horizon. New stresses emerged at work. Conflicts appeared on the home front. My happiness was short-lived, although I still experienced joy every time I helped someone, receiving their thanks. A few difficult patrons greatly stressed me. One in particular drove me over a cliff mentally. Soon I felt traumatized, even before recognizing it.

Hindsight is twenty-twenty. Retrospectively, I see my mistakes. I should have asked for help. I should have humbled myself by going to the local leaders to admit that one patron was too much for me. After dealing with her for two months, I began drinking daily, sometime in January 2018, just to cope with the stress and anxiety. Turmoil on the home front only added to my anxiety. I failed to cope in a healthy way. Looking back, I describe my mental descent as a nervous, emotional breakdown. Hence, my drinking led to my first DWI on Memorial Day, May 2018. Only after legal research did I discover the phenomenon of tiny stomach drinking that can quickly result in a powerful addiction.

# CHAPTER 51

# August 20th

## LETTER TO MY SISTER

Dear Lisa,

Day 96

I received your letter dated August 10th. Indeed, things are better. By the grace of God, I pulled it together, got over being mad, forgave, and resumed treating the ladies the way I would like them to treat me. Consequently, things are better; they are acting okay toward me.

I have been drawing lately, which began with requests. So with much practice, I think I am improving. Maybe that is all a part of the plan as well. There are no accidents.

I am pleased to report that things are good today. The chaplain told me after Recovery class last night that she could see the light and love of Christ in me and hopes I will join her Women's Bible Study classes on Tuesdays and Thursdays after I am released. That made me feel good.

Love you so much,

Shannypoo

PS: I like the card too, and the bookmark built into it is nifty. If it had been separated from the card, it would not have been allowed.

PPS: I appreciate your prayers for my potential early release. If that doesn't work out, I am probably looking at November 2nd as my out date.

# CHAPTER 52

# Monday, August 26th

## DAY 102: DENIALS

We are having more problems obtaining needed supplies. This time it is sanitary napkins. Several girls have heavy periods, and the tank's supplies have quickly run out before our scheduled replenishment. When we asked Ms. Connor for more, she denied us. Yes, the same CO who denied us TP chooses to deny us napkins, who also commands the other COs following her shift to not provide any. Headaches prevail among us; we submit written requests, but headache medicines are also denied for the same reason as always. Our floor bosses are in a bad mood. They feel that male COs who outrank them will not back up their disciplinary measures, especially regarding male inmates. The trustees are all fighting. I am recovering from being bullied, so I am not much help encouraging, uplifting, or consoling others.

Upon examining the calendar, I realize that I meet the requirement for potential early release, having completed two-thirds of my sentence, where I could be upgraded to three-for-one for overcrowding from the two-for-one time I have earned through work. My family and church are praying for my early release. I yearn for it fervently, given all the turmoil and negativity pervasive in the trustee tank. Meanwhile, I lost enough weight through fitness and lack of appetite to fit into a small size. I feel good, although I notice quite a few more wrinkles on my less-fat face. My semi-fasting is clarifying my mind, and I am beginning to understand the value of fasting for prayer.

# CHAPTER 53

# August 27th

## LETTER TO MY HUSBAND

Dearest, sweetest, bestest Husband in all the world,

Day 103

I miss you so much, baby! I can't wait to come home and snuggle with you! And Ellis, Bangles, Rocco and DeeOGee! Especially you, haha. I need to come home. I keep chanting, "I am home, I am home." I need my sparkling red heels to click together three times! I need to escape these flying monkeys!

Do you recall seeing a tiny young woman in the first booth Sunday? She's the one who possesses the secret potion to know exactly how to get under my skin and push the right buttons… She's the one prompting a good twenty-four hours' worth of tears when she begins shouting at me and cussing me out, causing me to lose my temper, and once that happens, there's no stopping it. I can't help myself, and the ugly that comes out of my mouth in response to hers shakes me far worse than her insults because I'm not supposed to be like that! Christ wouldn't do that! I want to be like Jesus! She makes me fail miserably! We all have talked to her about being polite, respectful, and considerate of others, but to no avail.

She's twenty-four, barely a year older than our son. And your mother thinks I did a bad job raising him! You spend twenty-four hours with this chick and tell me what you think then. You can't tell her anything! She knows everything! And she is usually wrong. She's got the disposition of a seven-year-old! Hard to believe all that out of a tiny little person, isn't it? If you noticed her. Her out date is mid-September.

Well, thank you so much, my darling, for letting me get that off my chest. Pray for me, my sweet. This has got to be the most difficult thing I have ever had to do, more so than the loss of freedom, feeling like I am back in high school under the mercy of those bullies twenty-four seven. I have no problem praying, exemplifying the Golden Rule, and forgiving. I told Christ I would suffer anything and everything for Him. Be careful what you say, right? Oh God, Lord, please have mercy on me!

Love you, miss you with everything I've got. XOXO,

Me2

PS: She's driving the rest of us nuts, not just me.

# CHAPTER 54

# August 28th

## LETTER TO MY SISTER

Dear Lisa,

Day 104

Thank you for your cards and continued encouragement. I hoped today would be my early release date at the latest, but the jail isn't overcrowded. I think I have served two-thirds of my sentence, but I miscalculated three-for-one, which would be September 6th rather than last week. I'm concerned about being kept here for "being too valuable." As inmate workers, we are currently down to four. The one with the most seniority is about to pull chain to go to another facility that is still a detention center but has a recovery program (SAF-P, statistically unsuccessful, but widely used in Texas over more successful programs, according to other inmates and one of the COs). I'll be left as the one with more experience; one other server is very new but will soon be gone, and one who is a cleaner only due to health reasons.

They'll probably roll in some newbies today. A very well-trained worker just got herself rolled trying to roll the other tank senior and me. Why me, I don't know, I've always been kind and good to her, and I like her, I never had a problem with her. Perhaps she had the mistaken notion that I prefer the tank senior, which isn't true. I'm not a game player; I hate these politics. Everyone is manipulative, back-stabbing, and a user. Well, not everyone. The cleaner isn't like that, and she won't take sides. I don't want to choose sides either. I wish we could get along in peace and harmony. They might mistake my kindness to the tank senior for preferential treatment when, in reality, I'm just trying to keep everybody happy, and if she's happy, it helps. If she feels excluded, we all suffer. Why can't they see this?

I dislike being ordered around, but I'm picking and choosing my battles to keep peace so I can just do my time and go home. So yes, the other tank senior is bossy, and I just do what she says because it's not worth the fight. Anything I try to change backfires. Nothing is worth the effort, like trying to share TV time and get people to be quiet when others are trying to sleep. Just having basic, common courtesy, manners, consideration, thoughtfulness.

The tank cleaner is like this; she's an excellent mediator when she chooses to be, but most of the time, she is quiet. She chooses to hang out with "the other side," though. I don't think she realizes that she spends more time with the younger ones, enjoying their preferred TV programming, joking with them, and so forth. I tried to be a part of their group and to keep the senior happy, but apparently, "playing on both teams" wasn't acceptable. I'm not good at being nice to some but not to all. That's not me. Never has been. Christ in my heart makes that even more impossible—to treat some better than others. So I'm basically on the outs again all the way around. So much jealousy, and over what? This is all meaningless in the long run.

I had no idea I'd be signing up for Survivor as trustee. It's really juvenile and ridiculous. I love and care about all of them, but the one who departed today leaves without knowing that

I sincerely cared for her. I see myself taking one for the team by keeping "tank boss" happy. That has worked somewhat. She made an effort to be more considerate because I included her.

How much more of this do I have to endure? Have I really been such a horrible person to be going through this? The good that came out of it was that when the two young ones were complaining about the senior and me to the COs, they were sent back in, and I was called out to work instead, and I realized for the first time ever that I am appreciated... I worry too much that I goof up, forget stuff, or am too slow and therefore disliked, but in actuality, having a pleasant personality coupled with a respectful countenance counts for a lot.

Yes, that's the good that came out of today's painful squabble. I thought I was probably in trouble and going to be yelled at, though, for what I didn't know; as far as I am aware, I have followed all the rules, behaved well (can you imagine me otherwise, big Sis? Haha). It's true that at fifty, I'm more forgetful. It's harder to recall that tank such and such has eleven, and another has seven, etc. It changes almost daily anyway. Special trays aren't too hard to keep up with because those with approved special diets are usually in here longer.

At any rate, my heart is breaking all over again for failing Jesus in shining His light and love to bring comfort to every woman I am housed with. Actually, these days, in this regard, I feel like a total failure. I'm trying to remember the ones who went away feeling more positive from our interactions. One girl released did write to me in here; that really touched me! We all exchanged addresses, but one actually wrote to me! Yes, I must focus on that and all the positives instead of today's trials. In the meantime, I'm going to keep praying for early delivery from this tumultuous environment.

I haven't been writing as before. Forgive me if I repeat myself. I don't know what I have written to who—ha!—I can't remember, but I sent all my writings and correspondence to storage (a secure bin stored elsewhere with my belongings in it) because one of the younger ones (who are still in here for a few more weeks) kept insisting I let her read it… Even when I explained it was like a private diary, etc. I worried about potential snooping when I'm out of the room or asleep, so just to be safe and keep my privacy, but hopefully, that wasn't really necessary. I'm not assuming one way or another. Her continued requests made me nervous.

It's great to write all this out. I obviously have no one here I can talk to, and even if I make a phone call, I can't talk freely. There is no privacy. Of course, staff review letters, but just for subversive content, and they're professionals who probably aren't worried about tank drama anyway. I can just imagine how old this gets! LOL. It's odd to me, I'm tired of it after three and a half months, and you may be as well! But thanks for "listening" anyway!

I've been practicing drawing instead of writing, save for letters, so I'm still productive. Requests began a month ago, so I'm improving with practice, so I'll draw something for you. I've made quite a few by now, but I don't think I sent you one yet.

Right now, the girls are speculating that there's a camera in here randomly taking pictures, and a voice recorder, up in what looks like a fire alarm. I think there must be a built-in sprinkler, but they don't think so… Would we not have a sprinkler to put out fires to be up to code? And having pics taken in an area where we change clothes, go to the toilet, and shower naked doesn't seem right. These women. Always one drama after another.

Well, I have to wrap it up now. As the jail turns, stay tuned for the next episode, haha.

Love ya always, big Sis.

XOXO, Shannypoo

# CHAPTER 55

# August 29th

## LETTER TO MY HUSBAND

Dearest Husband,

Day 105

I need to practice drawing animals as well as people. Not sure I can accomplish landscapes with a safety ink pen. I am using this extra downtime to hone artistic skill.

Can you see if you find *The Book of Mysteries*, which is a daily Christian devotional? One of my Sunday school students has been sending me a few xeroxed pages at a time, but the book is excellent. I can't remember the author, sorry. It's probably recently published. It has wonderful explanations of definitions and translations from ancient Greek, Hebrew, etc.

There are more shake-ups in here... people upset, angry, rolled, probably new ones coming in. Tank senior is still here. I just do not understand why there always has to be so much drama. Why can't we just be happy? We can't go anywhere anyway. Why does it have to be so hard to get along? I miss just being around guys.

I love you and miss you so much! XOXO,

Me2

PS: I just can't get our dogs quite right. I'll keep trying, though.

# CHAPTER 56

# Friday, August 30th

## DAY 106: TALL TALES

The longer I'm here, the harder it is to cope. I am so tired, drained like psychic vampires are sucking out my life energy and positive focus that I had when I first came in. I'm feeling very alone. Not abandoned by God, Jesus, family, friends, or my spiritual family at church, but I feel physically and psychologically alone. I realize my desire to run from the situation is the same that caused me to run from every difficult situation in life. I beg God to deliver me from this evil place.

My main problem is that Tammy has latched on to me a month after Jan's departure. In the meantime, I observed her rude behavior, being mean to new trustees, demanding respect she will not show. I tried speaking with her about the Golden Rule and how, if one exhibits desirable behavior while shining Christ's light, seeds are planted that bloom in others. *Very simple*, I keep thinking. *Treat others as you want them to treat you, and they will treat you as you want them to. I have seen this for myself, over and over.* Tammy is a difficult case. She must be the type Jesus refers to when He says, "… this kind goeth not out but by prayer and fasting,"[88] having so many spirits or demons in her. Sometimes, I see the woman emerge in her what God intends her to be, but rarely. One example of this is her complimentary support of my art. She asked me to draw her several times, her husband, and other family members from the photographs she has on hand. She is happy with every drawing I did for her. She insists I need to make my living as an artist. No one is *all* bad, the same way no one is *all* good.

After Ruth left I moved to her bunk, next to Tammy's, as it is supposedly a more desirable spot for watching TV, away from the toilet and phone. Soon, I began seeing what Ruth was talking about and felt repelled by Tammy. Recently, Tammy maneuvered herself into a position where she is able to drive a wedge between the other women and me, causing one relationship to completely fall apart, and, once again, I was blindsided. Tammy is masterful at her game, and this young woman, who goes by "Baby Shark," abruptly departed, rolling herself out while feeling bitter toward me, not understanding my current position.

A few weeks ago, I moved back to my original bunk. My official reason was to have more light by which to read because the lights stay off much of the time. The considerate COs keep them off so we can sleep between shifts. My need for light is true. My original bunk is closest to the emergency light that always stays on. Actually, I need space from Tammy. Her negative energy is draining me profusely.

For a while, this move helped. I felt relief away from Tammy, and I bonded with Baby Shark. Tammy, the mastermind, though, was fully aware of the situation. She found out from her last court date that she is moving on to her next destination, not home as she hoped, but to SAF-P, as part of her sentence. She believes she will "pull chain" quickly, so she stopped ordering commissary. We pray for her that she is right and will be gone soon.

Then, Tammy convinced Baby Shark to swap bunks under the pretense that Tammy needed to escape the noise of the younger women's chatter taking place to her side and above her. In reality, there is no escaping any noise in this room, which bounces off the painted brick walls. Tammy's move effectively put herself between the other women and me so she can create a physical and psychological wedge between them and me. The move brings her close to my commissary and gives her control over me and the others an impression she and I share a new "closeness." She lies to them when I am out of earshot about what I say and how I feel about them. She lies constantly. In the beginning, they were skeptical of me, but I think they are awakening to her modus operandi.

Perhaps her "tall tales" have clued them in. I secretly nicknamed her "Tall Tale Tammy." We giggle over her stories, such as the one where a spider laid an egg sack in her buttock and baby spiders hatched inside her. Another is about asps multiplying prolifically by touch, forcing her to move to a new residence with her husband and family twice. Or the time, not so humorously, when her husband supposedly knocked her so hard in the head that her eyeball popped out into her hand! The horrific abuse she is supposed to have suffered at his hands includes a dislocated shoulder and collarbone and having bullets lodged in her back when he shot her. Her stories do not jive with the loving, cooing phone calls she shares with him nightly when she cries over missing him so badly and makes smooching sounds into the phone. We really do not know what to believe. I have watched them in visitation when they press their palms up against the glass, batting eyes and blowing kisses to each other. Possibly he does abuse her; I truly hope not. This is not a woman who acts fearful of him in the slightest. Tim and her husband have spoken occasionally as they wait to visit us, sometimes up to three hours. Her husband remembers Tim from the time his band played at the Hanger. Tim says he seems like a nice person, but one never knows what goes on behind closed doors. I am not downplaying domestic abuse. Only the number of incredible tales Tammy tells makes us dubious as to what is reality and what is fantasy, and Tammy is a sucker for sympathy.

# CHAPTER 57

# September 2nd

## LETTER TO MY HUSBAND

My dearest, sweetest husband,

Day 109

I have prayed for the Holy Spirit to come back upon me and once again put joy in my heart after such a long time... I'm so grateful. I realized my attitude was bad, and I needed to adjust it. I blamed everyone else for the bad moods and tensions in the tank. I didn't cause them, but I wasn't helping the situation by reacting with anger. I prayed fervently to God that He would restore my ability to love and to exude happiness despite all the tank fighting.

We are all human, and undoubtedly, I will still have bad days, but I am very grateful that today the Holy Spirit is with me and fills me with renewed strength, hope, love, and peace. I just have to take it one day at a time. I can't worry now about when I am getting out. I must stop obsessing over it. Thinking about being home only makes me feel miserable in my longing and homesickness. So I relax now and choose to give it all back to God. I will wait till things slow down and we are not overcrowded to submit a release date request so as not to bug them; they have too many requests to deal with.

Well, it's funny or weird that when you told me about your friend's DWI arrest, I had just begun working on a new version of the band logo that isn't so cutesy but hopefully cooler. I hope your friend got out. Everything will be fine. It's all according to God's plan! I love you so very much, baby. I hope I can make you proud. Give all your worries to God!

XOXO,

Me2

# CHAPTER 58
# September 8th

## LETTER TO MY HUSBAND

My dearest, sweetest, most loving husband,

Day 115

I'm just writing to say I love you so much. As you can see, I'm learning jailhouse art, not only safety pen ink but watercolors made with Cool-Off (like Kool-Aid), deodorant, candy wrappers, milk cartons for blue color, and magazine cover colors.

I can't believe I'm in a size small, dude! Like, not a tight small, a loose small. I'm shocked and giddy with joy.

I love you, appreciate you, and I sing your praises! Thank you for being such a wonderful husband! You are awesome! I'm so proud of how you have held it all together, darling. I'm very thankful to your family for supporting you and helping you through this difficult time. Just remember God has great plans for us, and things will get easier!

XOXO,

Your wife, Me2

# CHAPTER 59
# September 9th

## LETTER TO MY HUSBAND

My dearest Tim,

Day 116

I have been contemplating my situation, that I will be here until November 2nd-ish, and cold weather is approaching. This jail gets extremely cold, so I would like to purchase a second pair of long johns/thermal bottoms. I am already wearing them! The AC gets frigid at night. Another pair of socks, too. So if you get another large chunk from Dad, could you spare more than $50? Here's my wish list:

- long john bottoms
- socks
- lotion
- shampoo
- deodorant
- proteins
- coffee and other warm drinks
- toilet paper
- mouthwash
- oatmeal—keeps me regular

Pretty soon, the jail will charge me another $20 for my prescription medications. I discovered I don't like the beef/cheese combo sticks, but the twin beef sticks are okay. I am not a fan of any of the Brushy Creek beef entrees.

I demand nothing and will survive just fine without, just less comfortably, so don't feel any pressure! Don't approach Chris and Trish at this time, but if they ask, let them know. They already have done so much! Don't ask anyone. But if they ask, this is the standard list. I really appreciate you!

I know you are working extra hard and just barely managing, so no worries. Besides, I'm enjoying being so petite and don't have an appetite anyway.

I'm in good health. I just have a problem "going," but a nice meds dispenser helped me on Saturday; finally, after two weeks, she brought me some Citroma and gave me extra time to drink the 10 oz bottle since I have a 4 oz stomach. She's an angel, truly God's vessel. I don't think the rest of them worry too much about us, except maybe the nurse, but we rarely see her.

Anyway, it's all good. Eight weeks! We can do this! Yay! XOXO,

Sunshine, Me2

# CHAPTER 60

# Thursday, September 12th

## DAY 119: NEW JOY

Tammy left two weeks ago. The day I longed for finally arrived. We joked ahead of time that when she finally left, we would throw a party. When the door closed behind her for the final time at 3 a.m. on a Tuesday morning, we burst out laughing, which lasted for three hours. I'm not proud to admit that I was the first to applaud when the door closed behind her, causing the girls to laugh hysterically and to join in clapping.

Our joy lasted all day, into the next. Lauren and I still feel it. The darkness walked out the door with Tammy. I am so thankful because we were at each other's throats. The last few shifts we worked together (largely due to the fact that no one else wanted to work with her), we began yelling at each other in front of the girls in other tanks and in front of the floor bosses, who ignored us. I was surprised when the COs refrained from commenting or chastising us, even when I sarcastically called Tammy "floor boss" in one of our heated exchanges, to which Tammy hotly retorted, "Damn straight I am!"

Retroactively, I see this entire experience as good. Despite my joy following her departure, I love her. I love all the women.

I realize this is God's love flowing through me, that my human love is insufficient. I feel His love, compassion, and forgiveness for her. I feel all bitterness and resentment melt away now she is gone. This is a powerful lesson for me in learning to love or show God's love in extreme cases. God has not given up on her. Hopefully, the seeds He planted through me and others will eventually germinate, but He does give us free will, so ultimately it is up to her, as it is for all of us, whether we truly turn our lives over completely to Him, to His will, plans, and care.

Subsequently, I found a new confidence enabling me to relax with our floor bosses and to resume shining God's love and light. I survived God's boot camp, although, at times, I nearly lost my mind. Testimony I received after Tammy's departure restored me and brought a new peace, empowering me to reconnect to the Holy Spirit. Now I feel joy in the Lord in my current environment regardless of negative, challenging personalities. One of the new trustees we received after Tammy's departure reminded me yesterday of the ability God gives us to feel joy in His presence at all times. I feel this way now after the worst I experienced. Trial and conflict truly bring us closer to Him. These experiences gave me epiphanies about scriptural meaning, deepening my understanding of His purposes, making our relationship closer and more intimate.

I met wonderful women this summer. The two who came in two weeks ago brought new opportunities for growth. One in particular reminds me of a young Carrie Fisher, so I shall refer to her as "Carrie." She speaks gently of God's reminders, healing me from recent trials. She shares her experiences, to which I closely relate, as I do with many of the others. She is wise for her thirty years, despite the challenging and "dire" circumstances in which she now finds herself. She exudes a peace about what she faces that a person without God may lack.

Lauren testified that I inspired her own growth, which amazes me and brings me to tears. I witnessed her spiritual blossoming but had no idea I had any part in it because we fought so much. I was in pain from our conflict and shed many tears. I went to a very dark place, during which Lauren and I shouted at each other, sometimes using foul language. What came out of my mouth was a first for me, tearing me apart, more so for what I said to Lauren than her words to me. I cried many hours afterward, embarrassingly sobbing through my evening shift. The floor boss compassionately let me stay out and work because I was traumatized and could not face my foe. At the end of my work shift, the floor boss kindly went into the tank ahead of me and smoothed things over a bit. Then Kelli revealed herself as an extraordinary mediator, speaking with us both separately, helping us establish a bridge by which we could meet in the middle, form a temporary truce until we ironed out our differences.

Subsequently, I poured my heart out to Lauren, asked for her forgiveness, and admitted my own pride and arrogance. I adjusted my negative attitude. Before, I let my ego and pride win. After I faced this, admitted it, asked God to help me, heal me, and once again fill me with His Holy Spirit, the truce with Lauren enabled us to work together cooperatively. Not only that, but we developed a new friendship. We now laugh at how we were at odds. Lauren confided that from the beginning of our time together, she felt "jealous" of me "having a close relationship with God" and "having it all together spiritually" as a Christian. This admission astounded me. I replied that I certainly do not "have it all together." She added that eventually, I inspired her to seek God. She worked her way through *The Key to the Expect-*

*ed End*, attended church "services" given by the volunteer ladies (who baptized us earlier in the summer) from local churches and who come twice a week to share scriptures and pray with us as we sit on the floor just inside the vestibules. Now Lauren and I study the Bible with the other ladies, and she offers insights during group discussions. Over fifty days together, I witnessed her become thoughtful, considerate, and kind. Her testimony, therefore, touches me deeply.

Now that we are close, she has taught me how to create art with the "free," indigent deodorants and milk cartons. We enjoy coloring, decorating envelopes, and making colorful pictures of the girls (I draw, and she colors). All the girls encourage me to draw their portraits. I have drawn Lauren's several times. She and I enjoyed watching the Harry Potter movie marathon together. We like watching other programming that interests us both. We braid each other's hair. I truly love Lauren and will miss her on this eve of her departure. I pray many blessings over her and that with our Lord's strength, she will continue her path to healing, wholeness, sobriety and will allow God to work His miracles in her life to use her for His plans and purpose.

I just received my official out date of October 30th. I have seven weeks left, or forty-eight days. I am relieved and happy to be closer to release, but I have new peace and acceptance, whatever it turns out to be. I was anxious before, hoping for an early release, but I am no longer worried. Plus, it is easier to be here now that Tammy is gone! God's will is my will, whatever it is. I happily accept His will for me. I continue to take pleasure in daily scriptures study while praying, semi-fasting, and feeling joy in the Holy Spirit.

If God had "delivered me from evil" as I begged Him to a month ago, I would have missed out on meeting Carrie and experiencing the evolved, healed relationship with Lauren. Nor would have I witnessed Kelli's remarkable ability to calm situations, infuse them with love while helping those in conflict to understand each other's viewpoints. These women helped me more than I have them, I think. Indeed, much of this time "put away," I feared I failed God in His mission, but He continually speaks through the others, telling me not to think that way. Many reminders of positive thought come through those around me, including floor bosses.

If most likely, I am still here October 30th, no doubt it will be due to more women I am meant to meet, help, and learn from, further facilitating spiritual growth. Ultimately, I cannot regret this entire incarceration because of my relationships with these women, my resulting growth, and my personal work with God. Once Lauren departs, the remaining women, Carrie, Kelli, Betty, will be here for several weeks close to my out date, fortunately giving me further opportunities to learn from them, mature spiritually, to love, encourage, and to lift them up before our time together ends.

While Tammy was here, she claimed all the "best work assignments." Since she left, I finally have had these opportunities to assist the COs in new ways, which is sometimes fun. Amazingly, the CO who gave me so much trouble over the summer, Ms. Connor, is nice to me now. The other day when I assisted her with passing out the commissary, she complimented me. Whenever the warehouse sends extra product by mistake, usually the commissary lady unofficially gives it to the trustee assisting her. On this day, the commissary lady was working another floor. When it turned out that there was an excess of peanut butter wafer bars, Ms. Connor told me she was going to give them to another trustee in our tank who is indigent and without commissary items, rather than to me, which is customary. I responded that this was fine with me. "To tell you the truth," I said to Ms. Connor, "I received so much help from my family, I always share with the other girls."

"You are so sweet," she responded. I believe she was sincere in saying so. She has been kinder to me since the day Baby Shark rolled herself because it was Ms. Connor Baby Shark complained to that day about Tammy and me. Ms. Connor was the one who sent Baby Shark and Lauren back into the tank, calling me out instead. When I thought I was going to be yelled at, I knew it was Ms. Connor on the floor, so it was natural to assume I would be in trouble. However, Ms. Connor, who was training a new CO, simply turned to her and said, "We will have this one help us instead because she is so nice." I remember my jaw dropping!

Baby Shark went to a tank across the hall, where she still is, so I wrote her a letter. I had to mail it to her with a stamp since "kites" are forbidden. Baby Shark received my letter, and the next time I went into her tank to deliver indigent supplies, she ran up to me, hugged me, thanked me, and told me she loved me. My letter deeply touched her as I explained the situation with Tammy, how I was protecting Baby Shark and the others from Tammy, keeping Tammy placated, rather than taking sides against them as Tammy had them believe. I poured out my heart in this seven-page letter! One of the women in Baby Shark's tank who was already familiar with me, having been here all summer, said, "Shannon, you are the bomb!" That made me giggle. My letter, obviously, had been shared with the entire tank.

Word spread around about the pictures I draw on request. Consequently, I have been drawing pictures by request of women in the other tanks. I have to mail them the pictures, with postage of course, but it is worth the cost. I receive back touching gratitude, sometimes in person as I work, passing out commissary, etc., and sometimes by mail. In person, the women cry and hug me. Their letters are sweet and sincere. Most often, I draw an angel wearing the armor of God as Paul describes in Ephesians, and I write the scriptures on the back of the picture. We can all use prayers for protection in this place. If I have to mail it, I include an encouraging letter. I feel so much joy in doing this, seeing the comfort it brings. One of these angel drawings went to my Angel, of course, still here in the tank I was housed in before becoming trustee. Lauren colored it for me, of course.

# AFTERWORD

Much to my great surprise, I was released five days after my last entry of September 12th. What I hoped for and dreamed about I gave up on too soon. So resigned to accepting my fate of at least six more weeks incarcerated. I convinced my husband to replenish my depleted commissary supplies. Only a week before my out date, I received huge gift orders, all kinds of goodies, thanks to my sister-in-law, who almost went overboard in her generosity. I found it ironic I was released when there was too much to carry. I packed what I could but had no choice but to leave some behind, delighting my hungry tankmates. As it was, a kind CO, the one who brought me the Citroma, rummaged up two garbage bags for me, having so many belongings, including books, Bibles, my handwritten "book," letters, and cards.

My release on Tuesday, September 17th, 2019, was just two days after Lauren's. Jail staff does not give notice ahead of time when released extra early, as in my case, upgraded from two-for-one to three-for-one due to overcrowding, and in Jan's case, released extra early as part of her divorce settlement. However, there were indicators. The first odd occurrence that morning happened with a sudden influx of girls into the trustee tank, including Raven and Baby Shark, much to my utter delight! These girls gave us a full house, which should have alerted me. In fact, I wondered because the night-time COs had been dropping hints about overcrowding and how trustees were always given first early release by seniority. After Tammy left, I was the "senior" (although I never called myself "tank boss" as she had. All I asked anyone new coming in was to be polite, respectful, and considerate of others. I never became "bossy," at least in my opinion).

I was so delighted to see my two old "friends" back, I jumped up and down, clapped, laughed, hugged them, and cried, "Party!" I thought about how the next few weeks were going to be fun with all the extra snacks, card games, art creation, and hair braiding.

Carrie was "needy," being indigent without family to buy her commissary and put money on her books for phone calls. So my next clue came after she asked me if she could use my account to make a call. I agreed but asked her to keep it short as my balance was low. She attempted to make the call and notified me that my balance was zero. I thought, *This must be it, I'm getting out!* The jail always transfers account balances to prepaid debit cards just before release. *Oh my! I don't have much time!* I thought as I went to my bunk and began sorting through my things, choosing what I must take and what must be left behind. I made quick decisions, routing some food items too big, bulky, or heavy to carry into Kelli's basket because she had very little. She was the most generous, though, with what she had and the most grateful for what she received. Whenever I snuck items into her basket, she declared upon discovery of them, "Shenanigans!" Hence, I adopted this new nickname, affectionately bestowed upon me by sweet Kelli, excellent arbitrator and most loved woman in the tank. Everyone loves Kelli and wants to be close to her. I quietly went up to her now and whispered, "I'm getting out." She looked at me dubiously and said, "Keep dreaming!" I just smiled. Moments later, the anticipated voice boomed from the speaker, "Teichmann! Pack up ATW, ASAP!"

Confirmation of imminent release thrilled me. I jumped up and down for a second time that morning, clapping in excitement, accompanied by astonished expressions from my companions, followed by hugs and congratulations. Grateful Carrie had asked to use my account for a phone call, I was prepared and ready when they came for me. With a last bittersweet look back, tears pricking my eyes, I said final goodbyes and exited the trustee tank. I only felt regret that I would not get the time with Raven and Baby Shark, after all, to catch up with them and to enjoy quality time with them all.

Several hours later, the jail was still processing my release. By the time I made it to "dressing out," several hours had passed. The jail seemed to be in an under-staffed chaos. I dressed into my last court-date outfit in minutes, but no one came to examine my basket, which was unceremoniously shoved aside in the hallway between dressing out and booking. A CO told me to sit in one of the plastic chairs lining the walls leading to visitation and the glorious exit for freed inmates. I sat there for an inordinate amount of time before my favorite medicine-dispensing CO came by, spotted me, and said, "What are you doing sitting there? Aren't you released?" Shrugging, I responded, "I don't know."

She checked and came back, saying, "Well, you are out. I'll escort you." She helped me accumulate my stuff into the trash bags and then walked me to the exit along with another favorite CO. She said, "I will really miss you!"

The other one said, "Me too, but do *not* ever come back!" I agreed, cried, and then went through the gate to freedom.

Out on the other side of the doors, I found myself momentarily alone in the lobby. I visited the ladies' public restroom and then tried to call my husband. However, the public phone would not call his cellphone, as it was considered long distance, and the system was prevented from incurring extra charges. By now, it was 7 p.m.

I meandered back to the lobby, where, luckily, a woman stood nearby. She held a cell phone, so I asked her if I could borrow it. Kindly, she agreed. Thankfully, I can remember two phone numbers by heart: my husband's and my son's. I dialed my husband.

"Locksmith," he answered.

"This is Shannon."

"Okay," he said. "How can I help you?" Of course, he did not recognize the number.

"Well, I am borrowing some kind lady's cellphone, calling you from the waiting room here. Would you like to come and get me?"

"Huh?"

"I'm out. I can't call you from the wall phone, won't let me call cellphones…" Silence. "I'm your wife. I'm borrowing a cellphone. I've been let out. Just now. Need a ride home. Can you come get me?"

Finally grasping who was calling him, he choked out, "Really?"

"Yeah."

I heard a sound like a gulping sob. "Okay… will take me a bit. Hang tight. Be there as soon as I can."

"Okay."

"See you soon." Click.

I handed the phone back to the nice lady, thanking her profusely for her kindness. She said, "No problem! Good luck!" and walked out the door.

I hauled my heavy load out the front door to the outside entrance in order to enjoy the last vestiges of sunlight (at this point, it was eight hours after exiting the trustee tank) and fresh air. I sat down on a concrete bench to wait for my husband's arrival, which took another forty-five minutes. A male inmate emerged from the jail, sitting on a bench across from me. We exchanged greetings. He was nice. He was incarcerated for a much shorter amount of time than I was. He waited for a ride too. He spent some time on his cellphone. I did not have my phone. My husband had kept it along with my purse when I was incarcerated. I just enjoyed being outside, looking around. I considered offering one of my candy bars to him and talking, but I felt too shy.

Finally, a dark blue charger pulled up. I called back to the other freed inmate, "Good luck!" He smiled and waved, and I ran to the man emerging from the car, jumping up into his arms easily, a light size six, 130 pounds slim, all muscle after eating very little and working out constantly. I wrapped my legs around his waist, kissed his face, and declared, "I'm finally free!" He laughed.

Tearfully and maybe a bit embarrassed, he then quickly ushered me into the car, depositing my bags into the back seat.

"Sorry it took so long to come get you. I had to drive my work car home. I wanted to pick you up in the charger."

"It's okay! At least you could come get me!" I smiled.

We drove home in twenty-five minutes of silence and felt the surrealism of the day sink in. I could not feel anything during the drive. What I imagined for months now melted away to thoughts of the women I just left behind. What could I do for them besides write? I thought, *If I receive any extra monetary help, I could send them books from Amazon or put a little on their accounts for phone calls.*

As we approached home, my thoughts turned to Ellis. Although I love all my dogs greatly, Ellis is the one who has absolutely eaten my heart. He cuddles with me constantly, shadows me from room to room, snuggles with me in bed at night. He is the one I worried about the most coping with being separated from me. I asked Tim to let him out first, alone, so he could have a few minutes to enjoy our reunion without getting knocked aside by the bigger dogs. Tim agreed and told me to sit on our swing in the front yard.

When he let Ellis out, he immediately spotted me, but from a short distance, he did not seem to recognize me, so he immediately began barking. I learned from this that he lacks good distance vision. His hackles went up, growling while he circled around in a wide arc, cautiously approaching me from behind the swing. I was surprised but amused he did not immediately pick up my scent and recognize me. Finally, when he was a few feet away, I said, "What, you don't recognize your mommy?" Upon hearing my voice, he broke out into a chorus of cries that from a human might sound like sobs. He jumped up onto my lap, licking my face, and I giggled while crying, "Oh how I missed you, my baby boy! You have no idea!"

---

Over the following months, I began typing up my handwritten entries for this book. I was unable to work on it constantly, especially when I read my notes from later in the summer when at my lowest point. At times, I could not face returning to the dark times. I put the book aside and worked on my art. I had some vague notion of beginning a new art career, but plans did not solidify in my mind until I was invited to show my art at a bridal exhibit in January 2020, which prompted my thoughts to crystallize into creating an art business. I was unsure what focus to take. I watched YouTube tutorials and joined Facebook art groups. Eventually, I stumbled upon pastels, with which I was unfamiliar but was drawn to and impressed by the beautiful, vibrant, stunning colors and details in pet portraits featured in the groups. Meanwhile, I honed my skills with pencil portraits of people. I drew people with graphite, in black and white or grayscale. I tried color lead pencils for pet portraits, which proved difficult. I failed to blend colors to make realistic-looking fur.

I realized pastels were key and began learning about pastel brands and the best paper to use. A special type of paper is required to make pastel particles "cling." I learned that Pastelmat is an ideal paper for the pastel "painting." Eventually, I obtained the recommended supplies and began practicing, doing portraits of my dogs and one of the barn cats, which turned out masterfully. At this point, I was in love with pastels, especially the pencil form, with which I seem to be more skilled than with acrylics and oils using paintbrushes. Consequently, I became determined to focus on pet and people portraits in pastels for my art business. My cat portrait eventually caught the attention of a cat lover who gave me many commissions, including his cats, friend's cats, and people as well. Through this discovery process, I learned how God's new calling for me as an artist could bring His healing through my art.

I spent several months apart from the book developing artistic skill, making business plans. Retrospectively, I wish I completed this book quickly, but I must trust God's perfect timing. I pray every day for opportunities to minister for Him however He sees fit; not the pulpit kind of ministry, but one where I can shine His light into the world, bring healing through His love, whether through art, writing, or simply in encouraging, comforting, and lifting others up. Hopefully, in viewing God as my "employer" henceforth, I can ultimately help, working with Him to bring others to Christ, that they may find redemption and healing through His great love and never-ending mercies.

As for the other women I was incarcerated with, Lauren, Jan, Francisca, Kelli, and I remain friends. I am unsure where Tammy is exactly, but she was back in the same jail twice in 2020. As of this writing, she is still in the TDCJ system. Ruth and I corresponded for six months until she was released to a halfway house from SAF-P, after which time I lost track of her. I often wonder about the others, and they remain in my heart and prayers always. Aside from Lauren, I am unsure if I was able to bring others to Christ or inspire them to seek God, but I believe He was able to plant seeds through me.

I do know that my faith got me through this tough experience and gave me a purpose and a reason for enduring this trial. Without faith and trust in God, my Lord and Savior Jesus Christ, I probably would have emerged on the other end psychologically traumatized. As it was, I experienced some PTSD, but continued Bible studies and growth as a young Christian have helped me to heal. Although I failed at times, overall, I believe God helped me to do as He instructed, shine His light and love into the darkest of places.

I hope that by sharing my story, this book can serve minimally as a cautionary tale to avoid making the costly mistakes I made. Hopefully, more so, it will help others going through similar trials by comforting, encouraging, showing how a relationship with Jesus is healing in His pure love. He is always forgiving when we repent and turn our lives over to Him. Even when we stumble and fall, as I did, we can always return to Him.

He brings so much joy and salvation through His redemption. He truly is the way, truth, and life.

# ENDNOTES

1   Doheny, K. "After Bariatric Surgery, Alcohol Abuse More Likely." *WebMD*, June 18, 2012. https://www.webmd.com/diet/obesity/news/20120618/after-bariatric-surgery-alcohol-abuse-more-likely.

2   Peterson, E. *Living the Message: Daily Reflections With Eugene H. Peterson*. San Francisco: Harper, 1996. https://catalog.loc.gov/vwebv/holdingsInfo?searchId=16199.

3   Jonah 1:17.

4   Matthew 16:19.

5   MacGill, M. "Oxytocin: The Love Hormone?" *Medical News Today*, September 4, 2017. https://www.medicalnewstoday.com/articles/275795.php

6   Matthew 5:42.

7   Columbia University Department Of Surgery. "Sleeve Gastrectomy: Center For Metabolic And Weight Loss Surgery." Accessed October 11, 2020. https://columbiasurgery.org/conditions-and-treatments/sleeve-gastrectomy.

8   Taubes, G. *Why We Get Fat And What To Do About It*. New York: Knopf, 2011. https://www.worldcat.org/title/why-we-get-fat-and-what-to-do-about-it/oclc/1091607682.

9 According to the Texas Administrative Code, Title 37, Public Safety and Corrections, Part 9, Texas Commission on Jail Standards, Chapter 285, Recreation and Exercise, § 285.1. Physical Exercise, "Each inmate shall be allowed one hour of supervised physical exercise or physical recreation at least three days per week."

10 Luke 6:29-30.

11 Furtick, S. *(Un)qualified: How God Uses Broken People To Do Big Things.* Colorado Springs: Multnomah, 2017. https://www.worldcat.org/title/unqualified-how-god-uses-broken-people-to-do-big-things/oclc/1050400559.

12 Richenberger, T. *Sold To The Highest Bidder: The Transformation Of An Exotic Dancer.* Scotts Valley: Desert Coyote Productions, 2012. https://www.worldcat.org/title/sold-to-the-highest-bidder-the-transformation-of-an-exotic-dancer/oclc/816093783.

13 Peterson, E. *Living the Message: Daily Reflections With Eugene H. Peterson.* San Francisco: Harper, 1996. https://www.worldcat.org/title/living-the-message-daily-reflections-with-eugene-h-peterson/oclc/1020203651?referer=br&ht=edition.

14 Our Daily Bread. Accessed October 9, 2019. https://odb.org/.

15 James 3:6.

16 Grissom, B. "Go Directly To Jail." *The Texas Tribune*, September 28, 2010. https://www.texastribune.org/2010/09/28/many-choosing-jail-time-over-probation/.

17 2 Corinthians 9:6.

18  1 Thessalonians 5:11.

19  Peterson, *Living the Message*, p. 144.

20  Matthew 7:1 (BSB).

21  John 13:34.

22  Souza, K. *The Key To Your Expected End*. Maricopa, AZ: Expected End Ministries, 2012. https://www.worldcat.org/title/key-to-your-expected-end/oclc/915635967.

23  Souza, *The Key To Your Expected End*, p. 46.

24  Souza, *The Key To Your Expected End*, p. 21.

25  Ripken, N., and Gregg Lewis. *The Insanity Of God: A True Story Of Faith Resurrected*. Nashville: B & H Publishing Group, 2013. https://www.worldcat.org/title/insanity-of-god-a-true-story-of-faith-resurrected/oclc/788256248.

26  Matthew 5:3.

27  Matthew 20:16.

28  Psalm 23:5.

29  John 8:7 (BSB).

30  Luke 23:34.

31  1 John 1:9.

32  Matthew 15:8 (NLT).

33  John 15:12.

34  Luke 6:27.

35  Luke 6:28.

36  Kerik, B. B. *From Jailer To Jailed*. New York: Threshold Editions, 2015. https://www.worldcat.org/title/from-jailer-to-jailed/oclc/1050300646.

37  Kerik, B. B., *From Jailer To Jailed*, p. 251.

38  Wikipedia. "The Bible (miniseries)." Accessed October 24, 2019. https://en.wikipedia.org/wiki/The_Bible_(miniseries).

39  Wikipedia. "The Bible (miniseries)." Accessed October 24, 2019. https://en.wikipedia.org/wiki/The_Bible_(miniseries). https://www.worldcat.org/title/four-agreements-a-toltec-wisdom-book/oclc/742420731.

40  Romans 3:13.

41  John 1:1.

42  Luke 23:34.

43  Matthew 6:15.

44  Mark 9:24.

45  Matthew 26:20-27.

46  Unable to verify or find any information about this possibility.

47  Reviews and claims of success rate varies according to location and source.

48  Reports on the effectiveness of SAF-P vary widely depending upon source.

49  According to the Texas Administrative Code, Title 37, Public Safety and Corrections, Part 9, Texas Commission on Jail Standards, Chapter 260, County Correctional Centers, Subchapter B, CCC Design, Construction and Furnishings Requirements, 37 TAC § 260.141: "Facility construction shall protect against the entrance and infestation of vermin. Materials and construction design shall contribute to efficient maintenance and housekeeping."

50   FEMA. "Hurricane Opal." Accessed October 14, 2020. http://www.fltf2.us/history/opal.html.

51   Eventually the church had to be torn down completely and is being rebuilt at the time of this writing.

52   Ephesians 6:11.

53   Auterburn, S. *The Life Recovery Bible*. Illinois: Tyndale House Publishers, 2017. https://www.worldcat.org/title/life-recovery-bible/oclc/1006470624.

54   Macy's Inc. "Macy's 4th of July Fireworks—The Nation's Largest Independence Day Celebration Will Ignite The Night Live from the Brooklyn Bridge." https://www.macysinc.com/news-media/press-releases/detail/1561/macys-4th-of-july-fireworks-the-nations-largest. "4K Macy's Fourth of July Fireworks NYC 2019 (GoPro View with 3 Barges) from Brooklyn Bridge Park." Filmed July 2019. YouTube video, 26:08. Posted July 2019. https://www.youtube.com/watch?v=GTljxHkZ8nk.

55   Strobel, L. *The Case For Christ: A Journalist's Personal Investigation Of The Evidence For Jesus*. Detroit: Gale Cengage, 1998. https://www.worldcat.org/title/case-for-christ-a-journalists-personal-investigation-of-the-evidence-for-jesus/oclc/927412370.

56   Strobel, *The Case For Christ*, p. 17.

57   Lea, J. "Former Police Officer Sentenced To 16 To Life For Murdering Wife, Hiding Body In Garage." *Mentor, OH Patch*, August 7, 2012. https://patch.com/ohio/mentor/former-police-officer-sentenced-to-15-to-life-for-murc6fa5479cf.

58   Habakkuk 3:18.

59 Souza, p. 44.

60 John 2:16.

61 Mark 3:5.

62 Nehemiah 5:6.

63 Psalm 118:14 (NLT).

64 Ephesians 6:12.

65 Luke 6:31.

66 Exodus 20:3 (KJV).

67 2 Chronicles 7:14.

68 Luke 12:10.

69 1 Corinthians 4:20.

70 John 11:25 (NIV).

71 See "The Widow's Oil," 2 Kings 4 (BSB). Accessed December 2, 2019. https://biblehub.com/bsb/2_kings/4.htm.

72 2 Corinthians 4:7.

73 John 7:38.

74 Hillenbrand, L. *Unbroken: A World War II Story Of Survival, Resilience, And Redemption*. New York: Ballantine Books, 2018, p. 236. https://www.worldcat.org/title/unbroken-a-world-war-ii-story-of-survival-resilience-and-redemption/oclc/1059486465.

75 Matthew 17:21 (KJV).

76 1 Corinthians 13:4 (NIV).

77 Luke 23:34 (KJV).

78 1 Peter 5:8.

79  Isaiah 6:3.

80  Psalm 84:12.

81  Ephesians 6:11.

82  1 Timothy 2:1.

83  Isaiah 53:5.

84  1 John 1:7.

85  Wikipedia. "The Bible (miniseries)." Accessed October 24, 2019. https://en.wikipedia.org/wiki/The_Bible_(miniseries).

86  Strobel, p. 222.

87  Ephesians 2:5.

88  Matthew 17:21 (KJV).